Downtown

Downtown

DAN RUSSO

iUniverse, Inc.
Bloomington

Downtown

iUniverse books may be ordered through booksellers or by contacting:

iUniverse
1663 Liberty Drive
Bloomington, IN 47403
www.iuniverse.com
1-800-Authors (1-800-288-4677)

ISBN: 978-1-4620-3466-6 (sc)
ISBN: 978-1-4620-3467-3 (hc)
ISBN: 978-1-4620-3468-0 (ebk)

Library of Congress Control Number: 2011911456

Printed in the United States of America

iUniverse rev. date: 08/02/2011

CONTENTS

Chapter 1: Downtown

If I had a time machine, I would wind up for eternity back in downtown Newark, New Jersey, in 1963. The years would reverse on my body, and I would know everything I know now.

I'd love to go back to the coffee shops and lunch spots like Schraft's and Chock Full of Nuts, Grant's Lunch and the Novelty Bar and Grill, Nedick's, Woolworth's Grill, and of course the Waldorf Cafeteria. God grant that to be my heaven for all time. How nice the people were then. The good times we had have never been matched for me anywhere, at any time, with any amount of money. It's a lost world I've never been able to find or duplicate since.

I guess downtown Newark of the early 1960s is my addiction, and I've spent my entire life looking for that fix.

It was a thriving, cosmopolitan city that drew shoppers and visitors from all around. The stores—Bamberger's, Kresge's, the huge Woolworth's—had wonderful smells of candy and homemade cakes and pies. The luncheonette loudspeaker would bark out: "Attention shoppers . . . there is no waiting for seats at our second-floor lunch counter . . . there you will find a choice selection of freshly baked goods and home-style foods . . . take the escalator to the second floor and enjoy your meal."

Hahne's, S. Klein on the square, and Orbach's were great, too. My grandma would buy a hat in Hahne's for a wedding she was attending, fold the price tag inside the rim, and then return it after the wedding. My gay cousin Liz tried to do the same thing at Orbach's with a suit, but the sales clerk said out loud, for everyone to hear, that he had worn it too long. He was so embarrassed.

You could find anything in the world in downtown Newark, from clothing to furniture to specialty foods. You could find super gifts for loved ones, and lots of places were open very late or even all night. And it was all a ten-minute bus ride from my home in the north ward.

Our relatives would come from the suburbs to shop there and used our house as their pit stop. This was a good thing for my mom, since she loved company. There was a standing rule: Don't bother to call. Just ring the bell and bring the cake for coffee.

But the best part of downtown Newark was the underground gay, bisexual, and lesbian scene my cousin Liz introduced me to. I'm not sure, but I might never have had any gay experiences if my cousin and I weren't so close in age. Without his influence, I would probably have been in the closet for much longer than I was, or perhaps forever.

I was in my late teens when my cousin came home one night and told me about the scene in Newark.

"Bobby," he said, using my middle name, "you've got to come downtown with me tonight. There are so many people like us. It was so much fun, and I met so many young guys who were interested in me."

And the next night I was there with bells on. Before then, between the ages of eight and eighteen, we thought we were the only two people in the world who did those strange and taboo things, like pull our pants down and play with each other. It was such a revelation.

We weren't freaks of nature as we had thought for so long. There were other odd people like us in the world.

Newark back then was truly the "gateway city," attracting people from all walks of life and from all over the world. It was a cozier version of New York, on a much smaller and more controllable scale. There were always transients who read Bob Damaron's guide to gay bars and nightspots and stopped by on their way to or from Manhattan.

There were so many gay and bi guys downtown that it was like our own city within a city. We loved using our own codes, lingo, and sign language.

The best thing was that most people who were shopping downtown had no idea of the underground world that was taking place right in front of their eyes. This same subculture has existed throughout time but isn't talked about. Most straight people, even the ones who thought they knew our scene, thought it was just a phase we were going through.

How funny that was to us. This was no phase but our reality for life.

I loved our secret world. All the signs, code words, and language, of which the straight world was oblivious, gave us a feeling of power and security.

There were words like "butch," which meant that someone was a manly type; "fem," which meant that someone was effeminate; "drag," which was someone who cross-dressed; and "number," which was anyone you had sex with or wanted to have sex with. Then there was "dish," which meant talking trash about someone; "gorgeosity," which meant he or she was simply stunning; "mop," which meant to steal something; "cruise," which was trying to meet someone for sex; "knocks," which was to get a beating from a guilty sex partner; and many more.

Of course, some of these words are common today, but keep in mind they originated as gay words many years before mainstream, straight America knew about them. I even made up a word that is mainstream today and has been for many years—the word "whacko" or "whack job" or "oh, he is whacked."

The local wise guys, who didn't see our scene for what it really was, had their own meaning of whacked.

The downtown area was so packed at night that you could get lost in the hustle and bustle. If a friend or family member saw you, well, you were just shopping or going to a movie or to dinner. We even had our own female fans who hung out with us and lent normality to our group. It was a great cover for people who needed anonymity. The cast of characters was amazing as well.

The Waldorf Cafeteria was the big haunt back then. The place was cheaply decorated, with a large front window and orange-and-yellow tables and chairs. What a fun place that was, with its fifteen-cent fries and twenty-five-cent burgers (real beef). Coffee was ten cents and pretty good too. I never knew how they made any money. The cups and dishes were "mix and match," but so were the ones we had at home, so I never minded it much.

The Waldorf had been there for many years and was always a "bohemian" hangout for the artsy types. They had a few Waldorf Cafeterias in New York City as well. The characters that hung out there were amazing.

There was Mad Alice who was always in semi-drag—that is, with the hair and makeup of a woman but in men's clothes.

Miss Coppertone, the older server at the Waldorf, always dyed his hair red and spoke with a lisp.

Mafia Bob wore a little hat and had a raspy voice, and what a nice guy he was.

John the Nazi was nasty and butch but as gay as they come. He liked to call me Hungry Hilda, because the hot numbers would always zoom in on me.

Lady in Blue always wore blue from head to toe and had this strange desire to get people mad enough to beat him up.

Then there was my friend Donald, who I nicknamed Eleanor Roosevelt because he was the spitting image of the famed first lady. He actually looked more and more like her as he got older.

Halloween was the night of nights at the Waldorf. It was the only night when all the effeminate or "fem" gays could cross-dress and be who they really were without Dick (perfect name) Spina, Newark's police commissioner at the time, arresting them all.

Spina was a tyrant with an ever-present bow tie and crew cut. He was driven around in a limo and raided the Waldorf regularly with his band of SS officers. Funny, but it always seemed that the closeted guys were the ones who harassed us for the whole world to see.

We were easy to harass because nobody cared about our rights back then. At the time, the strongest bonds were made between gays and IV junkies, because we were both considered outlaws and immoral types, the scourges of society.

There was this old, scruffy black guy called Mac who was a pickpocket. Mac wasn't gay or bi or anything; he was just another character who hung out there. He was a really nice guy, but he picked pockets for a living and did pretty well at it, too. Don't get me wrong—I didn't condone his line of work, but Mac was on a higher rung of the social ladder than we were. Gays were considered worse than a lowly pickpocket by the powers that be, and all of us knew it.

At the crack of midnight Halloween was over, and the Gestapo would invade the Waldorf and arrest people for impersonating females. It was actually illegal to cross-dress then, because you might lure an unaware straight male into having sex with you (*wooooo, not that!*). So off came the dresses and wigs.

During one Halloween downtown, I saw the whole drag thing play out through Liz. His real name was Ralph, but he thought he looked like Liz Taylor, the icon back then, always bragging that he had her violet blue eyes. This wasn't even close to true, but everyone called him Liz anyway.

We had nothing in common except for the fact that we were first cousins and both young. Within a few years, we stopped talking to each other for good. That suited me just fine because he had the brain of a minnow or more likely a no-see-um bug. But at the time we were bound together by our secret world.

That Halloween night Liz ran around my grandparents' house in a corset, pantyhose, and wig, and what a complete girl he was. My grandfather shouted in Italian, "What the hell is he, a female?"

My grandmother barked back in Italian, "It's that silly American holiday, where all the young people dress like crazy people. Drink your coffee and shut up!" She was always protecting my cousin, whom she had taken in as her own when Liz's mom abandoned him. Yes, my Aunt Helen left him at my grandparents' house like a stray cat because she wanted her precious life back.
I cared more about my dog than she did about her son.

Liz strolled into the Waldorf that Halloween night all dolled up, wearing my sister's gown that he had stolen from our house. The crowd roared, "Liz Taylor's dog!" An evil queen named Chickie, who sported an ever-present cigarette in a long holder, yelled out, "Call him Fido Taylor, Spot Taylor, Rover Taylor, but certainly not Liz Taylor!"

We all laughed and laughed. Looking back, I realize my cousin looked more like the comedian Ruth Buzzi of *Saturday Night Live*, which wouldn't be on the air for another twenty years.

I hung with the "straight" male hustlers because I was masculine ("butch") and didn't relate to fem queens. We would sit there every Halloween night and laugh at the drag queens as they paraded into the Waldorf. The fems always fired back, "You're half a fag. Why are you acting like such a big, bad man?"

The gay community always considered me "half a fag" because I wasn't quite "gay enough." I lived multiple, secret lives. Downtown I was gay, but I was deep in the closet at home, in the navy, and to my many political contacts. And I would stay in the closet until I reached my late thirties and early forties.

My answer was, "Because I'm a man, I have a dick, and I want to hang with other men. You act and smell and dress like a woman. If I want a woman, I'll seek out a real one, not freaks like you."

Life was always a better thing for me downtown, and except when the Gestapo showed up, peace was the norm. We didn't know of terrorists, and we always thought cheap gasoline and food would last forever. Diseases were minor and curable, and even the incurable ones were rare. The innocence and beauty of our country and world were special to us. You could be poor and still be happy and healthy.

We could go downtown and enjoy a full day of shopping, eating, and entertainment. And when that was done, we had the nightlife that would grow like a giant mushroom as the sun went down and the dark set in. And there it was, an army of spirits rising from the ground to stalk the night. There were no stalkers then, just overzealous men who wouldn't leave you alone because you were young and hot as hell. It was something to be thrilled about, not something to call the police about or a reason to put some poor guy in jail.

I loved watching men and women drool over me. I never fell in love with anyone, but I had my fun and played my games. I always made sure there was money in most of it, unless he/she was a super-hot new face. Then I might make an exception and give them a free

7

taste of that big Bobby action. Reminds me of another song: *"Oh the night life ain't no good life, but it's my life."*

The nighttime was such a thrill. I wanted to live entirely in the night and never see daylight again. And if it was raining, all the better, because I love the rain. The reflection of the neon on the wet streets and sidewalks looked like some artist had painted it there, and it made everything that much more exciting.

Chapter 2:
Childhood

I was the third of Rose and Daniel Russo's four children. Joe was the oldest, then my sister Rosemarie, then me, and then my younger brother, Paul. When I was a kid everyone called me by my middle name, Bob or Bobby, to distinguish me from my father.

Dad was an Italian immigrant, and Mom was born here of Italian parents. Dad's family had lived in Lyndhurst, a town just across the Passaic River from Newark. They were in the bar and restaurant business and did very well. I always credited them for my later success in the bar business, but who knows.

The north ward was the big Italian American area of Newark, but the east ward, a.k.a. the Ironbound, had a large Italian population as well. Called the Ironbound because it was surrounded by railroad tracks, it was also known as "down neck" because of its appearance on Newark's map. Talk about a melting pot. The Ironbound has had its share of just about every immigrant group to come to America.

My mom was from a large family of seven children, born and raised in Newark. They bore the full brunt of the Depression, with all of its horrors and struggles. Food was scarce for poor people like my mom and her family, and so were clothing and medicine. I believe that Mom suffered from maladies in her later years because of the malnutrition she experienced in her youth.

She would tell me how the family would eat hard bread with garlic, vinegar, olive oil, salt, and pepper for dinner. Then my mother would make it for us. That's now a fancy appetizer in many Italian eateries, and whenever I'm served it, I always think of her.

My mother would always tell the story about the butter and egg man delivering his products one day and Grandma Saporito telling him to stop the deliveries because she couldn't afford them.

The delivery man was Jewish and a family man, and after seeing my Aunt Jenny coughing away because of a virus caused by malnourishment, he announced to Grandma, "Madam, you have a sick child there. Pay me when and if you can, but take the eggs and butter for your children."

Mom never forgot that, and nobody could ever talk badly about Jewish people in front of her. "They're a lot like us," she'd say. "We're from the same mold."

My family grew up with many Jewish families, and the only difference I could see was that they encouraged their children to strive to be better and get a good education. Unfortunately, this wasn't the case for Italian kids because your parents wanted you married with children as soon as possible.

How my mother wanted children from me. I had the light eyes and hair like her mother. I sometimes think of who and what those children would have been and wonder if God is upset with me because I never brought them into this world. I often wonder if their souls were born through other couples, and I hope they were. It gets lonely being old and unattached without any children, but I have made a life of it, and it is my life now.

My mom and dad struggled, but so did most of our neighbors and relatives who lived in Newark. Everyone was poor, but everyone was nice and friendly. Blacks and whites respected each other's rights and privacy. You could walk the streets all night without fear that some drug addict would kill you for your wallet. Druggies were rare and not tolerated. We didn't need political correctness because we knew respect, decency, honesty, and reality.

Mom always said that Grandpa Giuseppe Russo was a wonderful father and businessman. He bought many homes in the Lyndhurst area of northern New Jersey for dust during the Depression and did well for himself. He remarried right after Grandma died. Then he died shortly thereafter, leaving all his money to Madalene, his second wife of a year or so. The rest of the family got nothing. I guess that was the macho thing to do back then. I found this out from conversations I overheard, since my grandparents died before I was born.

So Madalene lived a good, long life on our inheritance, while the rest of us struggled.

I found it funny that Dad and his siblings spoke of Madalene with respect. I would have contested the will and gotten her to give our families some of the money (or at least bad-mouthed her to anyone who would listen).

My father was a tool handler for Worthington Pump in Harrison, just across the river from Newark, and Mom was a housewife.

Our house was a three-story wooden frame walk-up, probably built in the late 1930s, with an old coal boiler that had to be fed every few hours during the cold New Jersey winters. Dad put us to work screening the burned coal to salvage a few unburned pieces. We shoveled coal ash onto a sifting device and then turned a crank handle round and round. It made more soot than it was worth for the few lousy unburned coals it rendered. It was child slave labor at best, and I hated it. If we didn't do it quickly enough for Dad, he'd use one of the curses from his native town of Salerno, Italy, such as, "You should get a disease of the eyes." Mom would scold him that it was wrong to say that kind of thing to children. I held my breath and kept turning the crank, ending up with white ash all over my clothes and also, I would imagine, in my lungs.

Money was tight, as Dad took home less than thirty-two dollars a week. Although we had a two-family house, between the mortgage and the monthly bills, there was never anything left. There were always strange families moving in and out of our third-floor apartment, with their children and their problems and secrets. Dad once threw out a young couple when he found them to be "living in sin." The man's wife discovered them living there and rang our doorbell to tell Dad, something unheard of today, for no one would even care.

Dad had a mean streak and didn't care who he hurt most of the time, but he did cry one Christmas morning after beating me with his belt. I woke him by yelling at my younger brother Paulie, and he actually apologized after he beat me, saying, "Daddy is sorry" with tears in his eyes. But that was the only time he ever apologized. He beat us mercilessly with his belt, and if we pleaded with him to stop, he'd simply respond, "Please is dead."

He had a bad habit of using that belt with all his might, buckle side out, taking out his frustrations with life and his struggles to keep us fed.

Dad also used a cat-of-nine tails. Of course, like most of what Dad had, he made it himself. One day we hid it in the oven, and when he turned it on, our plan succeeded. The cat-of-nine tails melted. Not skipping a beat, Dad went down to the cellar and while whistling an old Italian tune that I can still can hear in my head, made a bigger one with even more tails.

Oh, the good old days!

I had a lot of anger toward my father, but I didn't dare act on it. I always wanted to hurt him, but I was just a boy and my older brother Joe was no help at all. All Joe cared about was his own ass, even though he was a tough guy and could have easily put Dad in his place. He only did it once, and he did it the wrong way. He should have reasoned with him, told Dad not to be so old fashioned and crazy. But instead, when he and Dad were arguing, Joe hit him right in front of us. Dad put his head down and left the house. That was Joe—all for himself and his ego, not handling it in the way that would have been best for the family.

I'll never forget the cruelest thing Dad did to Paul and me. He had gotten us a beagle that we named Beno (Italian slang for head, because he had the nicest head and face). That little dog was the cutest thing I ever saw, and I loved him dearly. My brother and I would laugh and play with Beno for hours, which would aggravate Dad to no end. We even concocted a fantasy world where Beno had a wife named Emily and some kids, along with a Disney-type play land appropriately named "Beno Beno land." I made up a song to fit our fantasy world:

> *Fly away, oh fly away, to Beno Beno land,*
> *with Beno Belle and Emily, and all the gang is there.*
> *They'll take your money, pocket it,*
> *and throw you in the gas room.*
> *So fly away, yes, fly away, to Beno Beno land.*

Enticing, huh?

But Dad liked the house to be quiet and noise-free, kind of like a cemetery. Barking dogs and fantasy songs weren't his cup of tea. So one night while we slept, Dad took poor little Beno (who he never allowed in the house unless there was heavy rain or subzero weather) up into the mountains of West Orange (where we would have our picnics in the summer) and let him go.

He told us he brought Beno to a farm, but I knew better because Mom, through her tears, told me the truth. Winter was coming on, and that poor dog didn't have a clue about fending for himself. It broke our hearts, and we cried for weeks. Mom was so upset with Dad that she actually told him so, which was rare because he was quick to use the back of his hand on her. He just ignored her and kept eating his dinner, which I thought about poisoning. Then, after he was dead, I'd transport Dad's body to the mountains, where Beno could survive the winter by eating his flesh. But I decided not to do it. The poison might also harm Beno, and besides, how would I ever get Dad's body up there?

Mom knew it would affect us in some way, and she was right. When I brought up that incident years later to therapists, I realized this was the reason I couldn't let go of relationships and couldn't handle the loss of a close loved one or friend. I thought of poor little Beno for years and still do. I always hoped that someone had found him, took him home, fed him, loved him, and kept him warm and safe.

Yet, no matter what, I have to admit that Dad loved us, despite his rough and tumble old world style.

Mom, in contrast, was a saint. She always had kind and gentle words for us, and many ways of showing her love. Her smile radiated honest affection, and many people took advantage of her easy ways. It hurt me to see that happen, and I tried to educate her when different people talked her out of money. But she would always smile and say, "Oh, that's okay, they don't mean to do it. They're just hitting it rough right now." If Mom had three dollars to her name, she'd give it all to you if she thought you needed it.

What great Italian cooks Mom and Dad were. They could make something wonderful from a few meager ingredients.

As they cooked, they'd put down each other's families. Dad joked about how Mom's family thought they were still royalty back in Benevento, calling them "the royals" in a teasing way.

"Why don't you talk about your sisters," Mom shot back, "with those big, fat, high asses of theirs?"

We always had a vegetable garden in the backyard all through the summer season, and we canned much of it to get through the winter months.

If I didn't want to eat something my dad had prepared, he'd grumble at me.

"Someday you'll be looking for this dish," he'd say, "and if you can find it, you're going to pay a lot of money for it."

Boy, was he right, and I have to admit that remembering his words still brings a tear to my eye. (Well, except for the eel and watching him eat the eyes out of a sheep's head with a fork. Yuck!)

He also had an annoying habit of making us go to bed as early as 5:00 p.m. if we didn't eat everything. I always thought it was a big power trip on his part.

Family and friends stopped by unannounced if they were in the area, knowing that if they arrived at dinner time they'd be more than just welcomed. They would have a great meal.
The tradition was to always bring cake when you came to visit. I always looked forward to the visits, as well as the cake and conversation.

No other house in our tightly knit family and neighborhood had the draw or reputation that ours did, and I loved it.

When we could afford it, we ate homemade pastas and sauces, greens, fish, and meat. When money was extra tight, the children got the meat, and Mom and Dad, because they loved us dearly, ate string beans and potatoes. My parents wore old and tattered clothing so we had something decent to wear to school. They cared for us beautifully with what little they had and never complained. They made those wonderful meals with hardly any money.

I've never forgotten that. How many parents today would do that?

That's why I miss my parents so much and love and honor their memory. When I cried once thinking of them, Hank (my ex) said I shouldn't. I replied, "Honor thy father and thy mother," and he shut up.

And yet I hated my father's mean streak. He hit my mother if she said something he didn't like.

Sometimes he'd come home from work late. Mom knew he was screwing around, and she'd be washing dishes with tears in her eyes. She'd ask him where he had been. His only answer was to smack her hard.

He once hit her so hard that he left her with a crackling noise whenever she moved her jaw. The injury lingered long after he died, which I found to be ironic.

Chapter 3:
Sexual Confusion

How scared and guilty I felt, being a bi-curious youth in those days. In fact, my youth has always haunted me. Dad seemed to know all about my little secret, although I could never figure out how. Maybe it was because he once caught me and my cousin Liz masturbating each other in the alley alongside our house when we were around nine or ten years old. But that was supposed to be chalked up to simple adolescent curiosity.

Dad was from the "other side," as Italian Americans would say about people who were born in Italy. That meant that he didn't have to tolerate all the new-world beliefs and could be a lot more old-fashioned. That was a serious problem—almost a curse—for a young, confused, and curious boy like me.

He'd have me help him with some fix-it project in the cellar, because I was the youngest at the time. Then he would give me an all-knowing stare while he sang an old song: *"Mary Lou, I love you."* He stared me down without blinking an eye as he blew the sawdust from his latest makeshift project. In his mind, it wasn't harassment. He was just letting me know that he knew. But other than singing that song and staring at me, he never said another word about it.

From ages twelve to sixteen, I would go out for Halloween with everyone else in my neighborhood. But I wasn't looking for candy.

I wanted to go after those pretty little witch females and hot little goblin boys in their late teens. Comfortable in my disguise, I fantasized about having sex with a few of them at a time without giving up my identity. As you can see, I had these feelings from a very young age.

When I was twelve, I worked as a shoeshine boy at Broadway Barbers in Newark, which was owned by Vic Macione. The opera that played in that barbershop was wonderful and gave me a thrill like nothing else. It shaped my desire for Italian opera when I was young enough to be influenced by it that has carried on throughout my entire life. The smells of the aftershaves and hair tonics were clean and brisk, a refreshing and eye-opening scent I always enjoyed.

Sometimes Vic would say weird things to me, like, "Don't touch your little dickie" or "I bet my dickie is bigger than yours," but that was okay, since I had latent tendencies and was already curious at that age.

One time when I was about fourteen, I was in Nutley, New Jersey, trying to earn extra money as golf caddy. I was waiting for the bus back to Newark and these older teenagers approached me and asked if I wanted to blow them all. In my head, I wanted them all to blow me instead. Nothing happened, but boy did I masturbate later on thinking about all five or six of them fighting over my dick and then taking turns with it. They were hot young men and—whew!—I wanted that to happen, and the few times it did with other young guys I was in heaven.

In those early teenage years, I experienced my first crush on another man. He was a counselor at the boys' club summer camp and was tall and lean. I'll call him "Sally."

Sally was a stud and had a habit of letting young boys sleep with him as he kissed them all over their faces. I watched from my tent, more jealous than upset. I was in my goofy stage, with thick glasses and bushy hair, so I guess I didn't fit Sally's desires. But boy oh boy,

I so wished I did. Having a young man in his twenties on his knees for me was a real fantasy.

I had these sexual desires for as long as I could remember, although at times I wanted to be in bed with a woman. Too bad I didn't pursue it more than I have, since I could have made a good husband and father. Sometimes I feel I've wasted my life by not trying that route.

My mother was homophobic just like Dad, not knowing any better, but unlike him, she didn't really have a clue about me. In fact, she probably went to her grave without knowing. The thing I remember most about Mom's enormous family is that they hardly ever made any comments about Liz and me. I was never effeminate, but Liz was a total girl, always playing with dolls. But no one said anything because we were family, and that was that.

My father's family also didn't make any comments, but we didn't see them nearly as often as we did Mom's side of the family. With Mom's side, we saw them every day, while we saw Dad's once a week or once a month. There were so many children on both sides that I don't know how we remembered them all. But we did.

Apart from being sexually curious and confused, one of the most embarrassing things I had to endure until age sixteen was bedwetting.

Back then I had to use rubber sheets and diapers because nobody knew that some children's kidneys didn't develop as quickly as the rest of their bodies. It made it very hard for sleepovers, etc. My sister and younger brother would call me "pee da bed."

And nearly every day my sister Rosemarie called me "quattro louike," which meant four eyes in Italian, because I wore glasses at a young age. She would form her fingers into circles and put them up to her eyes. This went on for many years until she got married and I made a nice babysitter.

Siblings suck.

School in the late 1950s and early '60s was tough for a sexually confused youth, and being an altar boy was a guilt trip in its own right.

I felt so dirty and sin-ridden. Did Jesus really damn people who had sexual desires that were different than the norm? Would I be sent to hell? Were we really as bad as murderers?

The nuns and priests were very kind and supportive, and there wasn't any of that pedophile nonsense going on. I never saw a priest do anything wrong or ungodly. They were all good and God-loving people who cared about our futures and our education. This only made my feelings of guilt more profound. Why couldn't I be like them?

Chapter 4:
Outed

In the early '60s I went to Barringer High in Newark, which was mostly Italian American then. It was right across from Sacred Heart Cathedral, which is one of the largest and most magnificent cathedrals in the world.

Back then, Barringer was a classic stone and brick structure with Palladian doorways. Of course, the local politicians couldn't make money by fixing its leaky gym roof, which gave us showers when we exercised on rainy days. So they later tore it down and built a plastic and aluminum abomination in its place.

There was one gay guy in Barringer who was so effeminate he could have passed for a girl.
His name was Neil M., and he was a *total* girl. But his family was "connected," if you know what I mean, so it was okay for him to "girl out," as we would say. Nobody would even dare joke with him about it.

Neil came to my bars years later, and we joked about his name. It had more to do with his religious family wanting him to kneel down in church than with his gayness. He was a nice guy.

But for anyone else, if you were curious you had better deny it. Most young people of the '50s and early '60s were taught that anyone with an obverse sexuality should be beaten up or worse, and many of them acted that out. All you had to do was joke about being gay or bi, and the response would be a sneer, clenched teeth, and a fist.

Somehow, many of my male high school classmates sensed my bisexual preferences and would make comments and flash their private parts in the hopes that I might show interest or at least approval. I was never effeminate at all, but I guess guys know these things.

I finally had to leave school when I did the unthinkable and actually took one young classmate up on his offer. He was Johnny Derange, and a cuter German American boy I never saw. It happened on the last day before summer vacation.

We went to his house, and he took his pants off. He tucked his very healthy-sized penis (oh, those German boys) between his legs to make it look like he had a vagina and started dancing like a female stripper as a forty-five record played Ike and Tina Turner's "Poor Fool" and "A Fool in Love." Johnny thought his penis tucked away would excite me more. I would rather have seen him dancing nude with his large pee pee flopping around and those hairless little buns.

Johnny went crazy on me and came all over himself. I asked him not to tell anyone, and his answer was, "Tell them about what?"

Well, when we returned to Barringer in September, so did his memory, and the whole school knew. But Johnny made it seem like I was this fag who attacked him and his angelic straight body, and he had to fight me off to save his virginity. So I had to leave Barringer and go to Boys Tech, where nobody knew me. One clown with a last name that was close to mine made some comments, but I wound up on top of him choking him and the school got the message.

In high school I got a firsthand taste of the bi-curious scene's darker side.

I knew this extremely large-framed, hulking classmate, Sean, for whom I had neither attraction nor interest. We would walk home together since we lived in the same area, about four miles from the high school. The school was mostly Italian, but he, like Johnny Derange, was not. I believe Sean was Irish, because the few times he did talk, he spoke about his love of Irish culture and folk songs. Those were the days when young people still had pride in their ancestry.

One day, as we got about halfway to my home, we passed this wooded area that we locals called "the seventy-seven steps," because that many steps took you down through the woods to reach a lower street.

With a wink, Sean asked if I wanted to walk down the steps and go into the woods. I followed him out of curiosity, because he never gave me any idea that he was gay and was always a guy of few words.

When we got into the thick of the woods, he asked me to take my dick out. I gave him a puzzled look but started to rub my crotch with one hand.

Sean then tossed me around, grabbed me from behind, and started to strangle me with all of his strength. I wasn't fully developed in height and weight, and he was overpowering my attempts to escape.

I screamed as loud as I could, which wasn't very loud because I was being strangled. But luckily for me, a man passing by heard us and yelled at Sean, "What in hell is wrong with you? Are you crazy?"

So of course, I expected my attacker to say to the guy, "Well, it's really nothing. I was about to kill a queer, that's all." Like he was about to step on a roach.

But instead, Sean made this huge sperm stain on his pants, which both disgusted and confused him. He ran away crying, jumping down the seventy-seven steps without uttering a word, never to be seen by me in or out of school again.

I believe this kid was some kind of serial killer in training, and if the man hadn't been there to yell at him, I would have been murdered for sure. In fact, I wonder if Sean ever graduated into being a serial murderer just to prove he wasn't gay, only to keep sperming in his pants and crying his eyes out.

I had a sore throat for the next few days, with red ring halfway around my neck. I excused it as an injury from a wrestling match gone awry. I never told anyone the real truth for fear of being blamed as "the gay one."

Over the years I became scared many more times, wondering if the latest guy was like the "sperm pants strangler," but fortunately for me, when I did have a confrontation, I could fight or talk my way out of it by being a man.

Yes, those were scary times for people like me.

I have to give credit to my brother Joe. He never knew about my sexuality until the day when my blabbermouth sister, being proud of me I guess, told him. By then I was in my late forties.

Joe confronted me with it, and I told him it was true.

"Why didn't you tell me all this time?" Joe asked. "Were you afraid to tell me?"

"No, I wasn't afraid," I said, "but ashamed."

Joe began to cry. Then he said, "You hold your head up high and never be ashamed of what you are. And if anyone fucks with you, they're going to have to fuck with me."

I didn't know anyone who wanted to fuck with Crazy Joe Russo, and I felt better about my life after that. I didn't care who knew and whether they liked or disliked who I was.

Joe had a loan shark friend known as Frankie Fu. He was a nice guy but if he loaned you money you had better pay him back with interest.

Frankie was in court and some guy was ratting him and other wise guys out so Frankie jumps up in court and screams "I told you guys we should have taken him out years ago" with that the prosecutor says excuse me Mr. Fucella but what do you mean by take him out?

Without skipping a beat Frankie barks back "well I didn't mean to dinner".

Chapter 5:
Cruising and Characters

Downtown Newark had so many cruising areas it was hard to keep up. Married and so-called "straight guys" would drive round and round to pick up young guys for anonymous sex.

I made money by sitting back and being a man for these lost souls from the suburbs

A major pickup spot was Newark's Penn Station, a busy commuter and Amtrak hub designed by the renowned architectural firm of McKim, Mead, and White in a mixture of Art Deco and Neo-Classical styles. It had unused tracks where gays would go to have sex, and we had constant battles with fat, old railroad detectives who hated us with a passion because we interrupted their coffee and donut klatches. Of course, I fought back, which they weren't ready for. The other guys would look at each other and say, with a gloating laugh, "There goes big Bobby butch again."

Let's face it. We were the outcasts of society. I remember an article in the *Newark Evening News* that described how Penn Station had become, in the reporter's words, "A sordid and frightful place where marauding bands of homosexuals terrorize the travelers."

That was us—the marauding bands—ha! Marauding? Do you realize what scale marauding suggests? There were twelve of us, with only three or four in any kind of "band" at one time. But it sold newspapers I guess.

How funny that seemed to us, but the story took its toll on our freedom, because from then on the old, lazy railroad detectives had to get off their fat, donut-eating asses and chase us away every night. Too bad the outlaws that hang out in rail stations today aren't as harmless and docile as we were.

Other cruising areas were Military Park and Washington Park, where you made believe you were waiting for a local bus while cars zoomed by to check you out.

The balcony of the RKO Proctor Theatre was also an action spot. The Treat Theatre and Little Theatre showed soft porn movies that made everyone horny enough to stroke each other and beat off in their seats.

The men's room in Woolworth's basement was where old men hung out for hours to meet young men. I once caught Liz with some seventy-five-year-old man there. Liz always reminded me of a cat in heat.

We called the bathroom at Bamberger's "two and a half" because it was on a stairwell between the second and third floors. That was a strange name and game indeed.

You'd sit on a toilet in one of the stalls, and after mutual foot tapping with someone in the next stall, slide your body under so he could have his way with you. Some guys would stay in there all day and suck off three or four men, but I didn't have much interest in it because I couldn't turn a buck (there was no money in that for me). Another hot spot was the Public Service Bus Terminal men's room.

Every night you could meet scores and scores of men from all walks of life, from off-duty cops to local bank presidents to aging lawyers and businessmen—men who were straight by day, but after dark needed young studs with big tools to pound them silly.

And that was me—big Bobby, with my blond curly hair, big hazel eyes, and lean football player build. I was their dream stud. I was told many times that I looked just like Fabian, the '60s rock and roll star.

I always had an unconventional way of meeting guys and girls. Friends would do stupid things, like take a few weeks to earn a guy's trust. Then they'd invite the guy over to their place to try on some pants that no longer fit them so they could watch the guy undress. Lame! All those different-sized pants you had to keep in stock!

I didn't waste my time. I came on pretty strong. I'd say to someone, "What's a nice-looking guy like you doing alone on a Saturday night?" Within twenty minutes of meeting someone I was attracted to, male or female, we'd be on the way to somewhere private. I always got what I wanted. I was always up front and direct with people, whether it was business, money, or sex.

One night on my way to the Waldorf, I met my childhood friend, Vinny F., and his affected, closet case cousin. I was decked out in a black leather motorcycle jacket and tight jeans (or dungarees, as we then called them), and Vinnie's cousin couldn't take his eyes off me or my pants.

I tried to out them by inviting them to the Waldorf, telling them about all the fun and action I had there, and of course putting on the bad boy gay act. But Vinny would have none of that, demanding that his cousin, whose name escapes me, stay on the bus with him and not give in to the temptation of bazuzu (meaning me, the devil). The cousin whined so loud in disappointment that I could hear him as the bus pulled away, blowing garbage and leaves all around. I never saw Vinny or his cousin again.

The Waldorf had some real Damon Runyon characters.

Miss Pekinese looked like the dog of the same name, and always called any man he wanted "broccoli."

Judy the Chimp looked like a chimpanzee, ears and all. I actually lost a very sexy boyfriend to him. I ran into Judy in 2008, and he was still a nice guy. We met at a wonderful little dump in Belleville called La Sicilia, which has the kind of food that Dad warned me I'd have a hard time finding. Judy and I talked, teary-eyed, about missing the past and all the good people we knew.

Freda the Bird Woman worked at Miss Haircut on Raymond Boulevard by Broad Street and got the name by once doing a dance at a party with parrots all over his arms and legs. One time Freda took a vacation to San Francisco. As she/he got into a taxi at the airport there, the cabbie turned around and said to him, in front of his mother and her lady friends, "Aren't you Freda the Bird Woman from Newark?"

Michelina (pronounced "mick-a-lena") had a major drug problem and eventually "went botz" (crazy).

Vickie Marlowe and Josephina were friends until Josephina had a dish to tell about Vickie. Then we gathered around the tables at the Waldorf to hear the latest gossip on Vickie. The stories ranged from how he hid pills in his huge nose when the cops arrested him for drug abuse to the time he claimed to be the night manager at a local downtown hotel. (Josephina was quick to let us know he visited Vickie on the job and found him cleaning the toilets.)

Of course, we'd push the issue by asking Vickie about his manager job. As he described his importance to the hotel's operations, Josephina stood behind his chair mimicking someone cleaning a toilet.

Miss Thing with the glasses and Cummara Joe (Italian for godmother) truly reminded me of an old Italian lady who just got done pressing the eggplant.

One black queen was called Miss Da Doo Ron Ron because he claimed to be the piano player in the song and was so animated he could have been a cartoon character

There were so many others, too many to mention. Of course, I gave most of them their nicknames, to the point where they started to call me the "name giver," which I guess is like the truth teller.

If someone from our crowd disappeared for a while and you would ask their whereabouts, the answer was always, "Oh, she went botz," and that was that. It meant he either overdosed on pills, committed suicide, was committed to an asylum, or God knows what. Then nobody would ask for any more information, as if it were taboo to ask about someone who went botz.

We loved our secret, close-knit world. We had so much fun staying out all night. You could walk home at three in the morning without fear of being robbed or mugged. Or you could wait for the ten-cent, Number 18 Independent Bus and only get harassed by the local police, who thought you might be an IV drug user and always made you show them your arms.

Chapter 6:
The Navy

My dad died of a heart attack when I was sixteen.

For a whole year the poor man walked around our house in a robe with this pained look on his face, afraid to exert himself in any way and fearing another attack at every step. He'd have about three mini-heart attacks a week.

I felt so bad and helpless, but at the same time, I'm sorry to admit, I was glad that he finally left me alone.

Back then they had no meds to regulate your heart or to clear your arteries. There was no bypass or stent surgery either, so they sent you home to die. Poor Dad would cry and say to me, "Bobby, take care of Mommy for me," and I kept that promise for sure.

And then he would say, "Wisen up, Bobby, sa no you are gonna be sorry," which translated meant, "Think smart, or else you're going to pay for your mistakes."

I was the last one to see him alive.

He let me out a few blocks from Barringer High School because I was ashamed of his old car. Then he went fishing in Branch Brook Park, which was right across from the school. I actually ate lunch in the park that day as I usually did, not knowing Dad had died in that very spot. A few hours later my brother Joe came to the school to tell me and take me home.

Brother Joe took the money we got from my dad's half ownership of a taxicab, a whopping $3,500, and left the rest of us flat broke. Joe didn't look back and didn't care at all.

I tried to warn Mom, but she was afraid of Joe, who had a tendency toward violence. I came home from school one day and looked for something to eat in the fridge; there was nothing but peanut butter and mustard. Mom shouted, "Don't worry about it, just go to school." So I said, "Sure, Mom, and what do we eat, my books?"

She cried when I said I was quitting school to get a job. But I had to.

My first job was as a stock boy with the local Woolworth's, and at sixteen I wasn't below seducing the young assistant manager dudes. They loved playing with me in the stock room during "lunch."

Now I was bringing money home every week. To this day, I don't regret going to work. I don't want to sound like a saint, but I cared about Mom and she needed help.

Brother Joe continued to use Mom and me whenever he could. For example, at one point he decided to become a bookie—but not at *his* home, of course. Our home was his bookie spot, and he took bets for horses, sports, and numbers on our phone.

I hated it, but Mom wanted peace. He never gave us a dime for using our home and phone, and when I bet with him and won a few times, he said I lost and kept the money. That hurt my mom to no end. He would brag to her about how he fooled me.

Eventually Crazy Joe got arrested and put in jail for a few years for that crap. I was glad it was over. Joe had a problem with everyone around him because, as one of his friends put it, he had to have it his way. If you wanted to walk straight up the hill, he'd insist that you go three blocks to get there because his way was "the best way."

Joe never gave us a night of peace. He constantly fought with Mom and my brother Paulie. He was always screaming, breaking things, hitting Paulie and my sister, and threatening Mom. Joe never hit me, though. He respected my intelligence, or maybe he knew I'd get him back quietly, if you know what I mean.

Anyway, after a few years at Woolworth's, the company transferred me to their large New York store in the Chrysler Building as a restaurant manager trainee. I wanted to be an assistant store manager and had no interest in restaurant management. Woolworth's had an extensive in-house baking operation, but I would rather eat those goodies than be responsible for producing them.

I was tossed around to a few New York monster stores and then got an interview with a big queen who turned me down because he saw me as competition. I realized my life was going nowhere, so I decided to join the navy in 1963 at age nineteen, and I'm glad I did.

It was said to be the gayest branch of the armed forces, although it's common knowledge today that there are more bisexuals in the marine corps because, just like me, real men want to be with real men.

One day some ancient lady who looked about eighty, with blue hair and a black netted hat, saw me in my navy uniform and tried to lure me back to her room at the St. George Hotel in Brooklyn. When I told her no thanks, she said, "Oh, I see, you're the kind of sailor who joined the navy for the uniform." When I asked her what she meant by that, she replied, "You know exactly what I mean" and marched defiantly away.

Why didn't she just call me a fag, like most of the women I turned down? I know for sure that a certain marine I used to date would have slept with her, "just to see the thrill in her eye," as he liked to put it.

The armed services had their own underground, but it was deeply closeted. First you had to get really drunk with your buddy. Then you'd get a room, because you were too drunk to go back to the base, and things would happen. Afterward short-term memory loss would kick in, and all was well again.

Once I was at the Ho Jo's on the Garden State Parkway in Bloomfield with my big-mouthed but lovable friend Bob Paladino. Bob loved my one-liner wisecracks. So in came a whole busload of young marines in full uniform.

Well, I followed a few of them down the steps to the men's room and zoomed in on the littlest and cutest Marine. As I stood next to him, I saw his eyes drop to my dick. He couldn't take his eyes off it, and he stood there a long time watching me stroke it. I looked over and saw he had a tiny tinker bell pee pee. We really couldn't do anything because he was there with all of his Marine buddies, so I went back to the counter and finished my coffee.

Bob asked me about it, and I pointed to the cute Marine who followed me upstairs. Bob asked if I saw his, and I replied, "Oh please, it was Princess Tiny Meat," which made Bob hysterical. He shouted, "Ha ha ha! Princess *Tinnnneeeeeey* Meat!" The poor little marine heard him and ran out of the restaurant. Too bad. I would have loved watching his cute face get all red as I gave it to him good.

At the time there was a new phenomenon at the Howard Johnson's in Union and Bloomfield, where straight or bi-curious couples would sit and watch the gay cruising going on. The females would get all giddy and excited watching a guy cruise her male partner. This was long before being bi-curious was in its heyday.

Four years in the US Navy, including Vietnam combat duty on the USS *Okanagan* and USS *Navarro*, taught me volumes about human nature and the human male. I learned how to act and carry myself, how to be diplomatic, and how to reason between right and wrong.

Yet, at the same time, I always got mad as hell that I went to war for my country but never had full rights as a US citizen when I came back because I was "different" in some ways (even though I was more "normal" than most). In our society you're either gay/bi, or you're an American military or political patriot. But you can't be gay/bi *and* also a patriot. Nope, that isn't acceptable. When it comes to sex and sexuality, America follows rules that only the most ignorant countries and religions do.

Back in the early '60s and continuing right up until recently, the US military services were homophobic nightmares that carried out witch hunts on a daily basis. Whenever homosexual activity was suspected, moles were sent in to "out the fags." We had at least one mole in our unit, and everyone knew. But the best part was that the guys would warn each other about the moles and witch hunts. Despite the homophobia that existed, even the straight guys would warn the gay guys because they were our friends and didn't want to see us get in trouble. I found that to be strange, since we were all supposed to be stone cold straight and have no interest at all in the male anatomy. But I've always found that the homophobes are always the ones who are afraid of their own sexuality.

If you were caught masturbating anywhere on a ship, you would get discharged. The reasoning was that if you were straight, you couldn't possibly masturbate or ejaculate while surrounded by all those male bodies. Who in hell made those rules? Probably a closeted discipline officer, like the one we had at the Brooklyn Naval Base. I knew guys who were discharged because when caught in gay areas of town by our own version of the pink Gestapo (the MPs), they admitted that they masturbated, and what's worse, they had sex with other men. These were good guys and good Americans, because the navy didn't draft. We were all volunteers.

When we were stationed at the naval base in Brooklyn, we'd get many of those Section Eight sailors who were caught doing the unthinkable. The Section Eights included mentally unstable sailors as well as gay or bi ones. Anyone desiring sex with a person of the same gender was considered insane. Getting caught having sex with a female was cool and just a slight embarrassment, but if you were caught with another man, you were considered a leper or worse. We were warned to be wary around those poor guys.

Meanwhile, lesbianism went on out in the open, but that was considered hot and sexy since every heterosexual man was sure he had the golden penis to turn them straight.

It was odd for me to be considered part of the straight ruling class in the navy since I was totally bisexual and knew all the scuttlebutt of the day. I got to hear everything—who was screwing which wave (female sailor), which sailor on base was getting sex from everyone, and a who's who of enlisted men and officers caught with other men.

I remember the worst example of homophobia I ever saw. It involved an enlisted man who was in the navy for life and served his country well. He was middle aged at this point and ready to retire with a nice pension, but he made the mistake of getting drunk and winding up in a New York subway system men's room. Back in the early '60s, the subway men's rooms were mostly action spots for gay and bi men, and lots of young and old businessmen hung out there looking for a little fun on the way to and from work. Some guys even had their wives or lady friends waiting for them outside who had no idea that their man had just done the down and dirty with another man he had just met minutes before.

This sailor worked in the same office as me, and boy did he get disgraced and ridiculed for getting caught and arrested along with those other nasty Sons of Satan. Then he got a bad conduct discharge, which meant that he wouldn't get his pension and served all those years for nothing. I guess it was a good way for the government to get all that work out of people and then say, "Oops, you're a faggot and a Section Eight whacko. Therefore, you lose and we owe you nothing."

He got not a word of thanks for all those years of military service and all that youth he gave up for his country. There was not even any consideration for the fact that he might have been in the subway men's room for legitimate reasons and got caught up in the action out of curiosity.

Chapter 7:
Nighttime at the Waldorf

There were just a few gay bars in Manhattan in the early '60s, and I knew them well. In all there may have been only four or five, not because they weren't popular but because the police raided them.

The Stonewall Inn on Christopher Street in New York's Greenwich Village was one of them. It wasn't a great place because there wasn't really anything going on but some drinking and dancing. Two men dancing together without a female? Oh no, not that! Blasphemy!

When I was eighteen, my favorite place was The Fawn on the corner of Washington and Horatio Streets. You'd think you were in a speakeasy from the prohibition era, because gay bars couldn't get a cabaret license, so dancing was not licensed or allowed.

Here was the routine, which I remember like yesterday. We would feed the jukebox (since disc jockeys were a thing of the future, if you can believe that) and take to the dance floor, which was surrounded by tables and chairs. If the local SS came to inspect, which they did all hours of the night (including weekends and holidays), we would simply move the tables and chairs back onto the dance floor and sit down. How did we know the raid was coming? The front door would flash the lights when the storm troopers arrived. When the SS left, they'd flash the lights again and, *swoosh*, we'd move the tables and chairs again and go back to dancing.

It was sad when the bars sometimes doubled and tripled the five-dollar entry fee in order to pay off somebody, because then I was too broke to go in. The Fawn also had a habit of shutting off the jukebox and saying it was drink time, so we all had to buy another round before they'd turn it back on.

For some reason, the bathhouses were never raided. I guess the SS didn't want to see all that homo sex action or catch the crabs, which were really the biggest problem then.

The bathhouses weren't my thing. I didn't like being in a place where so many others had been before me. I was more the *Star Trek* type—you know, to boldly go where no man has gone before. I met my share of hot young men at the baths, but even after the best conversation and the most intimate sex, the gay attitude kicked in and—here it comes, that word I hate—*next!* A half hour later you'd see that same guy getting it from another guy.

Although New York had its attractions, in my late teens and early twenties the call of the wild was downtown Newark. It was my place to be every night with all my friends. I was Bob the Sailor, and that was good because it was a manly thing to be. There were scores of straight young guys trying to make money by having sex with other men, you know, today's "gay for pay."

One guy in particular always caught my eye. He was Donnie Della Pella, and I was enamored of that young man: brown hair, sea green eyes, and what a beautiful body he had. All his friends thought he was there to get taken care of and make money doing it. But when his friends got busy, Donnie and I would sneak off to a local cheap hotel.

It was probably my first real fantasy about straight guys compromising their manhood. While I was having sex with Donnie, I'd imagine all the ladies who craved him watching and getting real upset.

Every weekend and on holidays I would get leave from the Brooklyn Naval Station, head home to Newark, and go downtown. There was a glow there that I can't seem to find anywhere today. I can't explain it, but it was magical. You could feel the excitement of the crowds when it started to get dark. We knew another fun night would unravel, with freaky and hot people of both sexes and many different desires.

Downtown had its share of female prostitutes back in the '60s, although I never knew how on earth anyone could go out with them.

There was Taxicab Judy, who weighed in at a rotund 320 pounds. The poor thing always had pimples on her face that she failed to cover up with cheap Woolworth's Rejuva makeup. And her cheap perfume. We called it "Night in Newark" or "Holiday in Hoboken" or maybe "Saturday in Secaucus."

But Taxicab Judy had her steady johns, mostly taxi drivers and truckers. She used to drag around her little four-year-old son, who she kept up to all hours of the night. His name was Randy, and I remember that he was always crying. Judy had no money and did what she had to do to survive. Family Services took Randy from her one night, and she was never her jolly self again.

Then there was Grandma Moses, who at more than seventy-five years old really had to be somebody's grandmother. The hottest young guys picked her up and paid her for oral sex. It must have been that "grandma nurturing" they craved, because she wasn't baking them a batch of cookies.

When they dropped Grandma back at Penn Station, she'd go into this wild conversation, hands flailing in the air, exclaiming that her son or grandson had dropped her off. She fooled nobody with her imaginary stories, but I guess it made her feel better.

The window ledges of Penn Station gave us a front row seat for all the action taking place.

Grandma Moses would get picked up by one of her regulars, carrying her old and dusty overnight bag. Then a trucker or cabbie would drop off Taxicab Judy, who'd scream, "Three dollars! Why, you cheap motherfucker!" as the cab zoomed away.

It was a real camp, and we would laugh for hours.

I would always joke that Judy's torn fishnet stockings were nothing more than "body lice holding hands." She'd stare at my crotch with adoring eyes and say, with a big smile, "Hi, Bob."

I was so straight acting that she and many others thought my gay thing was an act. They thought I was really heterosexual (I wonder) and that maybe that I would turn a new leaf for them. I took pride in my manliness.

There were also straight girls who would hang around the scene. We'd call them "fruit flies" or "fag hags." They were there for the fun of it all and because they enjoyed being around guys who weren't trying to screw them at every turn. Besides, many of us (although certainly not all) had great taste in fashion and the finer things, even though we couldn't afford most of it. The fag hags learned good taste from us and how to handle their boyfriends, too.

Jackie Douche Bag, a.k.a. "Death Woman," was another character back then who I still talk with today. Jackie had this gray, death-like complexion and was so skinny he looked skeletal. Jackie had a stroke about ten years ago and today is just about a paraplegic.

He was a window dresser in the big department stores in downtown Newark for many years. It was a design talent that gay people are very good at.

One time I accompanied Jackie Douche Bag to an interview at Bamberger's, a wonderful five-story department store that Louie Bamberger started around the turn of the century, and that had so many departments it belonged in Manhattan. Bamberger's symbolized a special era in Newark; to tell its life story is to capture the great Newark that was and that hopefully will someday return—a thriving city where movies were made, great symphonies were played, and larger than life personalities lived.

I was with Jackie when he was interviewed for his job at Bamberger's by a very old man, who had probably been there when they laid the cornerstone. Since Jackie was openly effeminate during the interview, the old man asked about Jackie's military service.

Not skipping a beat, Jackie said, "Oh no, I got a deferment."

Of course, the old man had to ask why. I rolled my eyes and braced myself. Jackie replied, "Well, it was simple. I got a sex change, had my penis removed, and confirmed myself as a lesbian."

The poor old fellow fell off his chair, and we ran out of the store laughing like crazy.

Speaking of funny stories, I had a wonderful lesbian friend named Judy. I always teased her about her humongous tits, which someone had named "The Guns of Navarone." She would chase me down the avenue or around the political headquarters where we worked, beating and cursing me. With each punch she threw I'd laugh and laugh and then plead with her to stop. I'd sneak into her bedroom and as her partner laughed, I'd rifle around her closets. When she asked what the fuck I was looking for, I'd reply, "Your dildos." And she'd say, "Russo, get the fuck out of my room, we don't use those things." Judy was always a big one for women's rights, so being the frustrated lyricist I am, I wrote a song for her to the tune of "I Am Woman."

> *I am Judy, hear me roar,*
> *my tits are too big to ignore*
> *as I drag my big fat ass*
> *across the floor*

Boy, did I get the black and blues for that one, as all our friends spit their coffee everywhere. Judy later admitted she was glad I at least picked her favorite song. My poor friend—she had a bad heart and didn't make it through the bypass surgery. I was so glad I sent her flowers before she passed away. I miss you, Sister Jude. God bless you.

Unfortunately, Judy's lifetime partner of some forty years or so, who was supposed to be respected and accepted by Judy's family, was left without a penny when Judy died, like most gay partners before gay marriage became legal. When a gay person died before all this stupid civil union crapola, the family made all the funeral plans and took all the belongings and money, including mutually owned stuff like furniture. Poor Phyllis had been Judy's housewife, just like my mom was to my dad, and like my mom, she had no idea how to get a job. After Judy died, a friend helped her get a job so she could pay her bills. How sad that people abuse gays because they know the law doesn't recognize them as human beings with legal rights.

Chapter 8:
Working Day and Night

After I got out of the navy in October 1967 at age twenty-three, good jobs were hard to come by and mostly went to the college educated. The majority of us were not college educated, but we did fine.

Even with my above-average IQ, I found it hard to get and keep a job because I was more interested in going downtown than working at some mundane job for some dogmatic, lame-brained manager, who relished the idea of lording over me just to prove he was smarter. In my arrogance I would eventually just walk away, saying something like, "While we're still friends, I'm going to say good-bye to you and your job." And I didn't usually have something lined up to replace the one I was leaving. But the thrill of seeing the shocked looks from managers and fellow employees was worth it. The son of one of my bosses came up to me after I quit and said, "You really don't care, do you?" I replied, "Nope" as I packed my car and drove away into the sunset.

When I think of all the employees I've gone through over the years, I wish I had employees like me. I'd get brow beaten for the slightest things and then work harder to do a good job because I had pride in myself.

For example, one night I was working the graveyard shift in the computer data processing department at RCA in Harrison, New Jersey. The employee responsible for the company's entire payroll called in sick. Mind you, this was the late '60s, and computers were big and slow. There was nobody there that night, except these equal opportunity dudes who hadn't a clue and didn't want one either. So the boss called and asked if I would "try" to do the payroll for him. I got my hands on the job and the schematic for it, and I did the payroll for that week.

Of course, all the bosses showed up early the next day because they knew for sure that Crazy Russo (crazy because of my extreme political views) couldn't possibly have done the job right. They were certain they'd have to do it all over again so everyone could get paid on time. Well, surprise! I did it perfectly. They asked how I could possibly know, not having done the payroll before. So I said, "Oh that. Well, it was easy. See, I just called on some elfin friends who owe me for not turning them into stone." As they laughed, I explained that I followed the schematic. They had a lot more respect for me after that.

I should have stuck with that job because I could have easily become a programmer and would be doing very well today, but I always followed my heart

RCA's graveyard shift was perfect for me because I would take the bus downtown early in the evening, hang out with my friends, meet up with a paying john or two, and at around 11:30 p.m. take the PATH train to Harrison and go to work for the night. Then, when my shift was done in the morning, I'd run into one of the regulars at Penn Station, like Transistor Sister or Mad Alice, who would tell me if anything exciting had happened during the night.

Perhaps Mac the Pickpocket got arrested again, and we didn't have enough to chip in and bail him out. Or maybe George (the Great Frog) had met this "gorgeosity" of a man who gave him a new suit from his store in Manhattan. I guess the Great Frog really used his talents that night.

Back in the early '60s there were no cross-dresser prostitute types to mention, but there were a few guys who openly dressed like women and had straight boyfriends who knew there was a dick under the dress. It never made any sense to me but they loved it, so who was I to judge? They would meet a lot of guys, or, as the drag queens would say, "The *numbers* you pick up in drag, honey."

They even had their own song to the tune of "Making Whoopee." It went like this:

> *A little makeup, a little paint,*
> *A little being something you ain't.*
> *Put on your dress now,*
> *You're such a mess now,*
> *'Cause you're a drag queen.*

I guess there are many types of guys who really are females in their heads and are tormented by being imprisoned in a male body. I knew a few transsexuals who managed to get the money to have the operation and become the woman they really were in their heads. One of them got into an argument with Mad Alice at the Waldorf one night. As Alice boasted he would soon be a woman, along with having his beard removed by electrolysis, Louie Brown (now Louise) said to him, "Oh, bullshit. You'll be doing men underneath the table until you're ninety-three years old." As of 1992, Louise Brown was right. Alice is still Al.

The whole transsexual or sex change operation was a long and drawn-out process back then. It would start with getting female hormone shots for at least eight months to a year, along with electrolysis and voice lessons. It was only done in the Scandinavian countries.

The first known American transsexual was Chris Jorgensen, who became Christine Jorgensen, the talk of the gay community. Of course, I never understood why any man would want to cut his dick off and become a woman.

One poor fool, George Ball, who I renamed Lucille Ball, wanted it so bad that he attempted to cut off his own dick one day and almost succeeded. We never saw him after that, so I figured he either got his family to finally pay for the operation or went botz.

My gay cousin Liz had always wanted to become a woman, but he never had the balls (excuse the pun) for that, or anything else, for that matter. He never even finished grammar school and couldn't read or write English. He would take my friend Eleanor Roosevelt with him on job interviews or to help him fill out applications for a home or car purchase. Sorry, but I never had any patience for that type of lazy stupidity. Born here and can't read or write English? What on earth possessed him? I always thought Liz was just plain lazy because I had it so much worse than he did and I learned to read and write.

I couldn't understand Liz at all, since he had the power of Grandma's money and could have gone through college. Instead, he chose to drop out of grammar school and be a dunce, living in constant fear for the rest of his life that someone would ask him to read something. (Well, I guess in a way that's good, because he can't read this book, and my dear friend Don, a.k.a. Mrs. Roosevelt, recently died, so Don can't read it to him.)

Grandma Saporito left Liz much of her money before she died, so my mother got screwed out of both her and my father's inheritance. Well, as the old Billie Holiday song goes (my favorite of all time), "God Bless the Child that's Got His Own." That song and a few others have made me strong throughout my life.

> *Them that's got shall get, them that's not shall lose*
> *So the Bible says, and it still is news,*
> *Momma may have, Poppa may have, but God bless*
> *the child that's got his own, that's got his own*
> *Yes, the strong gets more, while the weak ones fade,*
> *empty pockets don't ever make the grade*
> *Momma may have, and Poppa may have but God*
> *bless the child that's got his own, that's got his own*

How true—we were the weak ones then, and I knew I had to change all that.

Now, a story about "botz." My Grandma Saporito was sitting in her always unlit living room one night, holding one knee and rocking in her chair. My Aunt Jenny (Mom's best friend) and Aunt Helen (Liz's mom) were carrying on this long-winded conversation. But the only problem was that they were talking about two different subjects. Jenny was complaining about her favorite problem, namely her car, and Helen was complaining about her husband, who she called "mope head." I was very confused by this and looked at my grandma with disbelief on my face. Grandma had the perfect answer without even hearing their words.

"Eh patch!" she exclaimed, and I burst out laughing. So I said, "You mean you know?" And Grandma answered, "Yeah, I know. What am I gonna do? Eh patch!"

So I ran over and gave her a big hug and kiss. Of course, "patch" was a more correct way of saying "botz."

There was a certain comfort sitting in Grandma's dark living room and hearing those voices emanating from the shadows.

I was not without regular johns in my youth, but I didn't consider myself a male prostitute. I was just playing around and making some extra money for myself in those tough times, or at least I thought.

There was Five-Dollar Jake, who was a retired tailor and known to pay you five dollars if he could drink from the fountain of youth. That's what a lot of older guys wanted from younger guys. But he paid me a lot more than five bucks.

Bill, who my friends knew as Twenty-Dollar Bill, gave me hundreds for sex and spent thousands on clothes for me. Bill even got to meet my momma and started hanging around my family.

I went to his house once and sat in his dead mom's favorite chair. I got the feeling of someone pressing me down into the chair, and when I told Bill he laughed, saying, "I guess Mother doesn't like you using me for my money."

Chapter 9:
Secret Lives

Throughout most of my life I've led multiple secret lives, juggling work, home, politics, the navy, and the secret gay part. I had my sex life and then all these other lives going on, sometimes in the same day, without losing a step along the way. In all I led four lives—my family, the political world, gay and bi, and the navy.

I've always felt this disconnect between being bisexual and my many other roles in life that are so much more accepted. Being bisexual is about 10 percent of my day-to-day life, if that much.

But as you can see, I, like most guys, can't stop talking about the sex side of my life, and maybe it's because it was and is the most exciting 10 percent of our lives. It's the variety that sparks our lives.

I hope everyone who has honored me by reading my book will understand how torn I am between my political beliefs and my personal wants, needs, and freedom. I am truly tormented and constantly at odds with myself.

I grew up in a conservative Italian family, I'm a Republican, and I served in the armed forces. And I've also been a bisexual man my whole life.

I was always torn about my sexuality. All my life I was torn about it. Many times I wanted to drop the whole bi thing and just get married and have children. I was told so many times by other bisexual guys I knew that I needed to get married like they did and have a family because there was no future in anything else.

But I didn't do it because I didn't want to ruin some woman's life. That was what a lot of my friends did, because they didn't care about anyone but themselves. They got married but still had their secret male lovers on the side. And when AIDS came out, a lot of them got caught with their pants down (excuse the pun).

It was difficult leading separate lives, but it was also fun. The excitement of doing such intimate things with total strangers was my biggest thrill. We hadn't a care in the world because back then there was a cure for just about any STD. Guys always wanted me to have sex with them, and I loved the power trip of taking their manhood.

One night while walking from Penn Station to the Waldorf, I ran into two sailors in uniform. They said they were from the USS *Compass Island*, so I barked out, "Oh yes, EAG 153, huh?"

They got paranoid because I knew their ship's number and wanted to get on a bus back to the Brooklyn Navy Yard, but I explained that I had been stationed in Brooklyn. We wound up in a dark ally, and I fucked one sailor while he sucked off the other one, and the one getting sucked off kissed me at the same time. It was strange how complete strangers would usually do exactly what I wanted, without question.

Most people didn't know the real Dan Russo. Some people thought I was totally straight, some thought I was bisexual, and then others only knew me as gay friendly and nothing else. The gay crowd didn't know of my political connections, my involvement with females, my life with the straight world, and my family. And my family and most of my friends didn't know of my gay life. Some went to the grave, I'm sorry to admit, not knowing me at all.

Until I was in my late thirties, early forties, the only people who knew I was Bi were the downtown and gay bar crowd. My family had no idea. My political friends had no real knowledge. No one in the navy ever knew. I got out after four years with an honorable discharge. I didn't get caught doing anything because I didn't do anything unless it was off base or with some other sailor I knew and trusted.

When I came out, it was to everyone but my family. I came out to friends and political associates, and by then my brothers and sister knew, but the rest of my family was too old fashioned to handle it.

My sister, Rosemarie, found out after we visited my mother in the hospital. She simply asked me, I told her, and that was that. She didn't care. Paulie probably found out through the gay bar I opened. He didn't care either, unless he could benefit by using it against me.

Some people did use it against me. They tried to out me. They'd threaten to tell my family unless I helped them out in certain ways. And then I'd swing at them or tell them to go fuck themselves. I'd never let them blackmail me into anything. God blessed me with big shoulders, and I kind of let everything slide off my back.

A lot of people from all corners of my many lives thought I was seriously Mafia connected and involved. Of course, the more I denied it, the more they believed it.

Employees at my straight bar revealed that other bar owners would ask them how the Mafia would ever allow a sexually confused guy like me to run a successful straight club. I'm not going to go too far here but will only say that power perceived is power achieved and leave it at that. Or like Don Vito Corleone said in *The Godfather*, part one, "And then they will fear you."

Don't get me wrong, I was not without my shady friends back when I was young and hot, but they trusted me because of my ability to keep my fucking mouth shut, as well as for my other qualities, if you know what I mean.

One scary dude I knew back then always had his car trunk filled with priceless paintings and guns, but I never asked questions (which he wouldn't have been able to answer anyway, with his mouth full). But a cooler dude I never met and probably never will.

How I loved being a male escort back in the days when such a thing wasn't supposed to exist. So many powerful men had a need to fill, and I was glad to oblige them. The money was great for the early '60s, and I needed it badly. But another of my secret lives that no one has ever known about, except for a few dear friends who have died as of the writing of this book, is that I have had numerous one-night affairs with women.

The strangest thing about this confession is that it was the heterosexual part of me that I always kept a deep, dark secret. The reason why I feel it's all right to reveal this now is because so many heretofore "straight-acting men" have come out as liking other men, so if they can confess the truth, I think I can too.

Most gay men used to scoff at bisexual men. "Oh yeah, he's straight—straight to bed," they'd laugh, or "Yeah right, he's bisexual, he likes men *and* boys." Only recently have gay men accepted it because it's "Fendi trendy," and besides, they're getting more "action" than ever.

It's been a hard life keeping my different and adverse sexual preferences separate, secret, and apart for so many years, but at times it's been exciting and fun.

The many women I met in bars and clubs and on the road have always been in their twenties and thirties and have had a pretty but boyish look, usually with short, dark hair and not a lot of makeup. They were what I would describe as almost lesbian and manly. I guess manly females turned me on for obvious reason.

One affair I had lasted for five years. It began when I was forty-two and dating a younger man of about twenty-two. I went to the mall to buy him a Fendi travel bag, since he was going to California for his birthday. Funny, but he broke up with me as soon as he returned from the coast.

At the mall I ran into this pretty young lady in her mid-twenties who, of course, had a short, dark hairstyle. She complained that her boyfriend wouldn't allow her to swallow, so I took her to my car and dropped my pants so she could have herself a drink. It was so exciting for me to fantasize about both our boyfriends catching us that I continued to feed her the man juice for five more years. We would probably be doing it right up to today, except that her boyfriend or husband by that time did catch us and flipped out. He was cute as hell, and being the crazy fantasy freak I am, I had her ask him if the three of us could get together so she and I could sandwich him. But when he heard her request, his face turned as red as a Jersey tomato from shock and anger.

I always fantasized about getting caught. The fantasy is great fun, but the reality of getting caught is not fun at all.

Many times, as I led my secret lives, I wound up meeting strange characters.

One guy looked like Jason Alexander—you know, George Castanza from *Seinfeld*. He kept calling me after I met him, and I shook him off with a lame excuse that I hated because I don't like lying, but he wouldn't take a hint.

Another one got off a train at, of all places, Newark's Penn Station from Tawny Town, Pennsylvania. And I swore I saw red, white, and blue bunting on the train, because this guy was the ghost of Abe Lincoln. I put him back on the train before they shot him again, but not before he got super drunk for free at my bar and created the persona of a frightened turkey on Thanksgiving day with his wobbly eyes and poultry looks.

Still another was the spitting image of Nosferatu, the original vampire from Mallorca, Spain, with his pointy chin, nose, and vamp style (or Ming the Merciless, a la Flash Gordon) hairline. He sent me a ten-year-old picture of himself, so I sent him back to Mallorca with a pint of pig's blood (for a snack) I had snuck into his suitcase.

Oh yes, I forgot that another one came here from Florida and swore he had a porn star-sized dick. When he got his pants off, I knew he did porn films for the Elfin community. I just wonder what they're thinking when they send these very old photos of themselves or really hot photos of someone else's body and lie about their anatomy. Did they really expect me to believe and trust them?

And let us not forget the English lad who flew here for a day and then left, saying his grandma was dying in Florida. Then I got an e-mail from his brother telling me he's an AIDS victim who flies to America often to rob older men.

My mother's words always echoed in my head: "Bobby, get a nice lady and get married and have some children so you aren't alone in your old age."

Sometimes after falling out with a lover (male or female), I'd come home to my momma. She would sense the hurt in me and ask what was wrong. I'd always say nothing was wrong and that I was just tired. But she knew better. "But Mommy loves you," she'd say. "Always remember that."

I knew it was true, and that's what kept me from losing my sanity.

A momma's boy? Yes, maybe, but it was an unconditional and honest love that I never got anywhere else and never will again, now that she is gone forever. "Gone forever" sounds so cold and empty to me.

I do know, looking back at it all, that if I had left the nest at a young age for this lover or that, I wouldn't be the successful and strong person I am today. As one older, well-educated queen we called the Great Frog (because of his bug eyes and graveled voice) told me when I was eighteen, "Listen to me, Bobby and remember—as far as gay relationships between two men are concerned, at best it's a temporary thing."

His name was George, and he wasn't the nicest guy. But he was honest, and I always preferred honesty to niceness.

I now believe the statement that any woman can take any man away from any man, at any time, and for any reason whatsoever.

I will never understand why men in today's world have a hidden, secret side that their partners, family, and friends know nothing about. Yes, I led separate, secret lives, but that was in a time when being gay or bi was completely taboo. In today's world you don't need to live secret lives anymore.

But when some guys go out on the prowl, you better bring your pets inside and lock your doors, because they are apt to do anything with anything and don't care who they cheat on or eventually hurt.

Probably the worst case of secrecy and betrayal I have known is one Steve F. This little asshole used and lied to everyone around him and would sell out his own family for the right price. Everyone knew him as an open and out gay person who would do any man, anytime, anywhere. Then came AIDS in 1983, and Steve "decided" he was no longer gay. His cowardly heart couldn't face anyone with this horrible disease, which in his view God had given gays as punishment for lives of promiscuity.

So he concocted this wild scheme where he actually married a very wealthy man's not so pretty daughter and became an infamous advocate on how to change yourself back to being straight, putting down the whole gay scene, and insisting he had no desire to ever be with men again. The very moment his wife's dad died, he got his hands on the inheritance, and *poof,* he was gay again. Steve left his wife and child to run back to a world where AIDS was understood and treatable and it was popular to be gay again although when I googled his name on line I found he is still on the "I'm a former gay man" bandwagon.

If anyone ever deserved a permanent STD, it was Steve F. And if I ever run into him again, I promise I will bust his nasty, lying face wide open.

This little jerk off would cruise Washington Park every night and go with many guys of all walks of life and thought nothing of turning his back on anyone twice.

He's probably in some South American country now where nobody knows him. He hasn't got the balls to face the world after leading people on a charade that they could change their sexuality or their son's or daughter's sexuality. Not to mention the gay people who knew they couldn't change but had to face an intolerant world that thought they were only "acting" or going through a period of "insanity."

I would watch Steve on TV telling the world how he cured himself of homosexual desires, and I knew he was a lying little weasel. Gay activists caught him a few times in gay cruising areas, but he always denied it. I hate liars, but he was worse than just a liar because he said things that made people think that being gay or bisexual was a sickness that could be cured (if you really wanted to be cured). He tried to convince the straight world that gays didn't want to pursue a cure and were in denial about being gay. He set back beliefs about homosexuality at least fifty years. I hope you burn in hell, Steven F.

Funny thing is, throughout my entire life I have seen people like Steven F. get theirs right here on earth. They didn't have to wait for hell to get payback for their acts of cruelty and betrayal.

Chapter 10:
Italians and Food

As you know, I'm very proud of my Italian heritage, and one of the aspects of that heritage that I value most is the food and cooking of my youth. You could go to most Italian restaurants today and never find the wonderful meals that my parents produced in our humble kitchen, and I don't care how fancy or expensive the restaurant is. Speaking in Italian, they would instruct each other in different techniques they had learned from their respective families or argue about how to bread or marinate something. They never had to call anyone for cooking advice.

The food was always great (or as they say in Italian, *"saporito,"* meaning tasty. Funny, but Saporito was also my mom's maiden name). When it came to the meatballs with pasta sauce (or "gravy"), it was Mom who made the best gravy around. And that wasn't just our opinion—everyone in our family and all of our Italian neighbors had to admit that Rosie's gravy and meatballs were the best.

She'd start with two pounds of freshly chopped pork, beef, and veal, from our Italian butcher only. She would never use supermarket meat. Then she'd add two eggs, fresh chopped parsley and garlic, fresh grated Romano cheese, Italian breadcrumbs, and salt and pepper. She'd mix it and add more breadcrumbs until it had the right texture. Either too dry or too moist was no good.

Whenever we asked for an exact recipe, she always replied, "You judge, it's easy." But believe me, it wasn't easy at all.

If you want to make a good tomato sauce, here's how. Pour olive oil in a large pot to just cover the bottom, and then add half an onion and three cloves of garlic chopped fine and brown them (onions take longer to brown, so put them in before the garlic).

Then add your tomatoes. I use three boxes of Pomi strained tomatoes or three cans of Cento San Marzano peeled tomatoes, and one large can of Contadina tomato paste. Mom used three large cans of peeled tomatoes instead of Pomi, which weren't around then. After heating it for a half hour, add six to ten chopped fresh basil leaves from the garden.

Make the meatballs in your palm by closing your hand into a soft fist and removing the excess meat. Roll it into a ball and brown on both sides. Do not fully cook the meatballs—just lightly brown them on both sides. They will finish cooking in the gravy.

Brown two pork neck bones from the butcher, and after a half hour, add them and the tomato paste to the sauce. Let it cook for another hour, adding a cup of dry red Italian wine, and then salt and pepper to taste.

Here's the best part—let it sit in the fridge for a day so the meat soaks up the sauce. If you freeze it, it tastes even better.

Want a marinara sauce? No problem—just do it without the meat.

Okay, one more thing. If you want a crab sauce, brown the garlic and onion in the olive oil (please, forget the extra virgin baloney). Then put raw crab parts that you've soaked in a little salt for three hours right in the oil, shell and all, for just a few minutes. This will give the sauce a wonderful crab taste. Add the shelled crab parts to the Pomi, but skip the tomato paste. Cook for just a half hour.

Please don't add oregano to any sauce, since it then becomes pizza sauce. And no cheese in the crab sauce, either

There are a few secrets I will not divulge here, but don't worry. If you follow these directions, the food will be good, I promise you. Never buy jar or canned pasta sauce, since it is sour and not good at all.

We always ate our salads as a dessert after the meal, and Dad would make us drink a concoction of half homemade Italian red wine and half Seven-Up because, he said, it was good for the blood (right again).

We also had lentils and pasta made from scratch, almost like a soup, more often than I thought we should, but again, they were right about the high protein.

They had a wisdom that only a thousand of years of family know-how could pass down. It makes me proud to think about their knowledge.

The quality food I enjoyed as a child was gone in a flash when I turned fifty, because by then all the corporations had opened their so-called restaurants all over the world. These places are nothing more than glorified bars whose main product is liquor, so the food doesn't matter much. Places like Olive Garden, with their microwave dinners that everyone raves about, really burn my ass. I even know of certain alleged restaurateurs who take their families there because "it's cheap."

My all-time favorite is Romano's Macaroni Grill, which reminds me of someone grilling macaroni. Once I ordered the chicken parmesan, and with the first bite I was convinced the world had gone botz. It melted into a dry, powdery substance I had to spit out. But the waitress was oh so pretty and didn't bother to ask me if anything was wrong. She was so cute, so how could you complain?

Applebee's is a close second, with its miniscule shrimp and silver dollar-sized steak, both having the texture of rubber. After a while the crowds catch on and stop coming, so what do you think they do? They simply change the menu and advertise it as the "new and improved" Applebee's. But the only thing they really improve is their profit margin. Nobody knows like Domino's.

I prefer places like Taramina in Kenilworth, New Jersey, Patsy's (for seafood) in Fairview, New Jersey, or La Sicilia in Belleville, New Jersey.

The corporate world has ruined the American palate, or what little there was. Julia Child was a help, but we really need more Italian influence in the American family kitchen. People today will eat anything if you put it on TV and say it's cool.

Chapter 11:
Siblings and Scams

In my old neighborhood of north Newark, the local Italians would call a child by his first name and use his mom's first name as the child's last name.

There was this woman in our neighborhood who everyone knew as Anna Lotatte (pronounced "lou dade"), which meant Loretta in some obscure Italian paese. Anna's mom was Loretta, so Anna became Anna Lotatte or Anna from Loretta. So I guess that made me Bobby Rosaria or Bobby from Rose.

North Newark was a lot like Brooklyn with these Italian phrases and rituals. In Brooklyn they called young wise guys "shabeeps," and in Newark we called them "shabopes."

Anyway, Anna Lotatte claimed she was dying for over fifty years, but in the meantime she buried three husbands, four children, and at least two grandchildren. It was the funniest story going in the neighborhood, next to the one about Anna visiting my mom (a scenario that I witnessed firsthand, so I can attest to its truth).

Anna had a bad habit of being *"scoushtumade"* (pronounced "scoosh tu maad" and meaning without manners)—that is, someone who comes into your home and helps herself to your food. So into our refrigerator Anna went one day, looking at what we had and what she might want to eat. She then announced that we had a full refrigerator, which set off the *"maloyke"* or evil eye alarm in my mom.

When Anna left, Mom swept salt down the stairs to fend off the evil eye that Anna had brought to our premises. When Mom told our first-floor neighbor Delores what she was doing, Delores not only peed in her pants but all over our floor.

I'm telling this story because I had a brother who was Anna's male counterpart. My brother Paul (or Paulie, as we called him) was dying for years.

For instance, every time he went into the hospital, he left these pathetic, whiney messages on my business voice mail. Like Anna Loutatte, he was dying again and wanted to see my smiling face, because to see my face again "would be like seeing angels." And then came the line "Daniel, my brother," which always made me step back from the speakerphone, waiting for him to break into song. The message went on and on: "I am dying, my brother. I weigh four hundred pounds. I am going blind. My heart is failing."

I knew he was lying again. I had heard about his many trips to Tony Hot Dog, the local hot dog truck on Park and Lake Streets in our old neighborhood of north Newark. He'd buy at least a half dozen of those dirty water dogs with homemade hot Italian onions and a bottle of Manhattan Special coffee soda. Besides, my heart doctor (who Paulie got me to refer him to) always said he was doing well, except for eating like a monster. He should have been crowned the Guru of Generation X, but they wouldn't have respected him because he was too old.

Because Paulie always claimed to be dying, you had to go along with his schemes and scams. I called him the jargon meister because he knew the lingo for every trade on the planet but nothing else.

For example, Paulie would tell you that your computer's hard drive and motherboard were both "fried." That didn't mean it was true.

It only meant that he wanted to charge you "crazy money" to do what might be a simple reset or download. So he did the work, you were happy because your computer worked again, Paulie was happy because he got his crazy money for such a simple job, and the day went on without any problems. The fact that your problem was a time bomb that Paulie had set up the last time he was inside your computer didn't matter—it was all part of Paulieism.

And you can bet that Paulie would screw his own brother even more than a perfect stranger. Why? Friends and relatives were an easy scam because they trusted you more and let down their guard. And there was much less of a chance that your family would prosecute you. He'd walk right past my mom, ignoring her, and my mother, who was a feisty old lady, would say, "What does he think, that I died already?" All Paulie cared about was his source of income, namely the shabang bang computer he had sold to me.

Paulie screwed Mom and me every chance he got and then told people I was the one screwing him. Of course, those who knew Paulie never believed him.

He even used his kids to extract money from Mom, making it clear that he wouldn't bring them over unless she gave him part or all of her Social Security check. If Paulie didn't get the money, he'd extract his revenge.

Paulie would call Mom and say he was picking her up to visit his kids. She'd get ready and sit there, with a little too much rouge and a big smile that soon turned to tears when Paulie never showed up. Then I'd take her for a ride. I never knew why he did that, but since Mom was old by then, maybe he thought she'd forget.

Paulie the Righteous even got to destroy my relationship with a younger man when his son, Paulie Jr., found out that I gave the guy, an employee of mine, a Mercedes I had on lease. There were only a few months left on the lease, and the car had an original price tag of $83,000. Paulie Jr., who wanted the car, went crying to Paulie Sr., who then called the employee's mom and speaking anonymously as a "concerned parent," told her that I had already given two young men AIDS and that his son used to work for me and also had AIDS. He told her she should watch who her son associates with, and by the way, don't think he's driving that $83,000 car for nothing.

Well, Paulie recently died, and so I forgive him his atrocious lies.

The truth is that both of my brothers were always out for themselves.

I found out just recently that the allotment check I sent home to Mom when I was in the navy was used in its entirety to feed steak, shrimp, and lobster to my brothers and their fiancées. I had no idea that Mom was going hungry. Being the peacemaker she was, she never told me what was going on. How sad that is to me, and how angry I am at them for allowing that to happen. What looters my two brothers were. I will never forgive them for doing that to my poor, dear momma—never.

My dearest friend Tony took me from that slum of an apartment where my brothers left Mom and me and set us up in a beautiful two-bedroom apartment in the Roseville section of north Newark. He fully furnished it for us and paid all the bills for years. There were lots of new friends for Mom there, and with my brothers gone, we could live a life of freedom and respect without their selfish needs and demands.

Tony was the most generous guy I ever knew, even attempting to help Paulie when he was struggling with a young family.

Joe actually tried to come back once because he and his second wife were having problems. I said no way. He didn't like it, but he never tried that again.

Unfortunately, my situation is not unique. Too many children abuse and loot their parents.

I remember when Dad got very sick once and was on his back for a month or more. He couldn't work, and there wasn't any workman's comp then, so we had no income except for the rent we collected from the three-room apartment upstairs. Brother Joe, at sixteen, was of no help whatsoever. He was big and strong and got a construction job that paid pretty well, but he never gave our family anything.

One day Joe and I were standing outside while my mother was inside crying, wondering how we would pay the bills and get through the upcoming holidays. I had a paper route and didn't make much, but I gave what I could. Sis and my younger brother Paulie were too young to have jobs. But Joe had money from his construction job, and as he stood there with me, he pulled some bills out of his pocket and fanned them in his hands. Then, putting his upper teeth over his lower lip, he made a bug-eyed expression and this sucking noise I will never forget. It was like saying, "Oh well, I got mine, and screw the rest of you."

That was his attitude for the rest of his life, and I couldn't understand how he came from my mom and dad. Later in life, Joe sold books for the ironworkers union, a job reserved for "trusted made men," if you know what I mean.

That was the worst Christmas we ever had, or in reality, the Christmas we almost didn't have. There was no money, and we only got gifts because my Aunt Red (her real name was Rose, but she had red hair), who was Dad's sister, and Uncle Russ, her husband, bought them for us. They were nice people. But Brother Joe was nowhere to be found, and my mom's family avoided us like we had the flu—or worse.

Paulie managed to screw me when I helped him buy a computer school after he and a partner split up because Paulie robbed him. First I loaned him money to keep it going because he, his wife, and all three of his kids were on the payroll. Each had their own office with their titles on the door: Executive Director of the Urinal, Vice President in Charge of Sucking Blood from the School, etc.

Then Paulie claimed he was dying again with a looming heart bypass, so he sold the school to me after making huge loans and robbing anything of value. I expected it but not the next trick. He went around telling everyone that I stole his school from him because he was sick and then ran it into the ground.

To the tune of *The Beverly Hillbillies*:

> *Let me tell you a story 'bout a man named Paul,*
> *Screwed his brother with a school, and that's not all,*
> *Heard the sheriff was a comin' to his door,*
> *So he packed up his kin and they moved down the shore.*
> *Brick, New Jersey, that is.*
> *Trailer homes, cheap gas,*
> *Leave your wallets at the door.*
> *Y'all come back now, hear?*

Only once did Paulie do the right thing, and of course, it was in his usual loud and crude way. The feast of Saint Gerard was being held at Saint Lucy's Church, as usual, and I was running for the state legislature at the time. Paulie followed the statue through the streets of Newark barefooted, which was the tradition in honoring St. Gerard, in devotion to my election. What a scene that was! But of course, the local Democratic politicians had control of the saint and removed me from the platform because I was a Republican.

I left the house right after being honorably discharged from the navy. Brother Joe would wake me every morning, shaking my foot and shouting, "Yo, get out there and find yourself a job, man." Yeah sure, Joe. I'll go out there and get me a job so I can keep you and your fiancée in steak, lobster, and shrimp too.

So I went to live with a friend in California for about three months. It must have been like saying an incantation to a noisy pair of ghosts back east, because both my brothers left and got married within a few months of me leaving. That's when I moved Mom and me to North Twelfth Street in the Roseville section of Newark's Italian north ward. Mom was very happy there, and I made sure she was well fed and had tons of friends visit her. I even gave her a couple of credit cards. Of course, one of her desperate "friends" stole her wallet once and used them. You can always tell desperate people because their stomachs constantly growl.

If they can, some people will scam you repeatedly. They believe in their hearts that they're taking care of themselves and their families, and that God or maybe that big straw bird on the mountain will forgive them. But the road to hell is paved with good intentions.

Too many people have the goal of what the Italians call *"mangia mondo"* or wanting to swallow the whole world. And they are so greedy in their goal that they will destroy or gobble up anyone in their path.

The sad thing is that, having my mother's heart, I always try to help people. I guess I could pass as a sucker, but not really. I always try to save them from themselves or whoever is trying to harm them. But as they say, no good deed goes unpunished, and just like my mom, I have been punished throughout my life for my good deeds.

I still get the "Dan, you gotta help me" phone calls from panic-filled compulsive gamblers who are stuck in Atlantic City, broke, and with no way to get home. But I don't have the resources anymore and turn them down, telling them to call their own family members. It's annoying to get such calls, especially since most of these people never call me unless they need money. *I'm broke, so who's an easy mark? Dan, of course . . . yeah, I'll call Dan. He'll be stupid enough to send me more money to gamble with.*

These days I have a $200 limit plan when people try to get money from me. Here is how it goes. If their story about why they need a "loan" is good enough, I limit them to $200, which is all I can honestly budget now. Then, if they don't pay me back, which is the norm, I've bought them for $200. And if they try to get more from me without paying back the initial $200, I give them the old "Joe the Barber" story I learned as a shoeshine boy at Broadway Barbers in Newark.

Here's the story: Joe the Barber comes here from Italy and opens his shop. One afternoon, as Joe is shaving a man, Three-Finger Louie pops his head in the doorway and shouts out, "Hey Joe, can you loan me a twenty till Friday?" To which Joe answers in broken English, "Ma shu, Louie, go ina da drawer ova there anda you finda da twenty." So Louie goes in the drawer and takes the twenty, saying, "Thanks, Joe! I'll see ya Friday."

Well, Friday comes and Friday goes, and no Louie and no twenty-dollar bill. So, next week Louie pops his head in the doorway again and says, "Hey Joe, you got a twenty till Friday?" Again Joe says, "Ma shu, Louie, go ina da drawer ova there, you know where it is." So Louie goes in the drawer and says, "Hey Joe, there isn't any twenty in the drawer." To which Joe answers, "Oh Louie, you didn't put it back?"

Works every time.

When I became successful in business, it was like winning the lottery, and so I read up about how to deal with people who hounded you for loans. There are supposedly three types of such people. The first is the Paulie Connoli type, who will grab whatever he can, hate you because he had to do it, and never pay you back. The second is the Sarge the Leather queen type who takes a big, fat loan from you and has every intention of repaying you but never does and rationalizes why he doesn't or can't. The third type is the one I like best, because he/she hates the fact that "you got it," as they say, and doesn't want your money.

Why can't they all be like the third type? They all stop talking to you eventually, although the first and second types have often come back for a double dip into my pockets. What balls it takes to not repay a loan and then come back for another grab.

So I give them the Joe the Barber story, and they finally go away—at least for a while, anyway.

One last scam story. My brother Paulie's mother-in-law was Rose Grecco, whose photo was in the dictionary next to mother-in-law for sure. This woman would wreak havoc on you and your family just for the sake of attention or whatever else she could extract from you to get her to go away. One of her favorite scams was that she would fall everywhere and then sue for money. She did very well at this profession. Local restaurant owners locked their doors whenever a phone call warned them that she was wobbling down the street. It was pretty funny.

I remember she would knit these small woolen red-and-green Christmas wreaths to pin on other ladies. Every year I had to take my mom to Paulie's house for Christmas, and there was Rose with her red-and-green knitted wreaths, which I was convinced had a Sicilian *fattude* (or curse) on them. When we left Paulie's, I would remove the wreath from my momma's coat and throw it out while saying a Hail Mary. Momma knew what I was doing and would always laugh, but then in her special way she would say nice things about Rose Grecco.

Paulie called me once when he was visiting Rose in the hospital after one of her classic fall and sue incidents and explained how this tiny Filipino nurse had attempted to wrap a blood pressure tester cuff around Rose's arm. When that didn't fit, they brought in this cuff that Paulie said looked like it belonged to a rhinoceros or a hippo and proceeded, with Paulie's help, to wrap it around Rose's rotund arm. Then this tiny nurse used a foot pump to pump it up and it exploded, which caused Paulie to run from the room because he was laughing hysterically.

The best Mother's Day of all was when Mom, as usual, was all dressed up waiting for Paulie to take her and Rose to dinner. The phone rings, and it's Paulie's son, explaining that his father has the flu and doesn't want to give it to our mom, so therefore there won't be a Mother's Day dinner. Okay. I hung up and took my mom out to dinner.

Well, golly gee, as we passed a local diner, guess who was waddling in the door about to take one of her famous dives for money? Mother Rose, followed by Paulie and his family.

I guess old Rose was immune to the flu.

Chapter 12:
Gay Violence

I've always wondered why there was so much violence, drugs, and murder in the underground of the gay scene, in the past and now.

So many people were murdered because they were gay or because a person they had sex with became guilty and got worried about being outed. It almost happened to me a few times. A guy would have sex with me and then become violent and want to fight me, just to prove to himself that he really wasn't gay. I'd say to him, "Who cares? I'll probably never see you again." And that would usually put their minds at ease.

I remember a bad scene when I was twenty or so and walking in downtown Newark. A gang was beating up a young guy, who was screaming for help. So I got in the middle of it. Guys always considered me tough, and I chased them off just by charging them. Of course, the guy was grateful and cute as hell too. So being a good little sailor boy, I hugged him. The hug turned into a kiss, and the kiss led to sex. It was definitely his first time with a guy.

After the violent encounter with Sean the Strangler in my teens, I had another close call with death in the mid-1980s, when I went to a male hustler area of Manhattan, Fifty-Third Street and Third Ave.

There was a pick-up bar in the area named Rounds, where younger hustler types went to meet older businessmen for money. I had gone there a few times, but most of the young guys were hardened hustlers who had no passion or feelings, who didn't know how to be friendly or diplomatic. I tried to give it a chance more than once, but that New York know-it-all attitude was always in your face. The strange thing was that I saw some celebrities and famous designers there.

The close call happened when I met a very handsome young man on the streets near Rounds. He claimed his dad was a big attorney but wouldn't help him with school, so he was out there doing men for college money.

He was a hot, young English/Irish stud, and I had lots of fun with him before I dropped him off a few blocks away. As I was heading home, a young Latino male flagged me down. More curious than interested, I stopped and rolled down the window as he approached my car. He explained that he needed just ten dollars. He kept smiling a lot and coaxing me, so I let him in the car. We parked at the heliport, a favorite spot for gay hustlers.

Then he pulled down his pants. I didn't want him to touch me and told him as much. He then asked for more than ten dollars. When I refused, he put his arm around my shoulder like he was going to hug me. Then he cut off my windpipe, saying, "I already killed an old man here. I don't care. I'll do it to you too."

I managed to wrestle him off and started my Saab, which had the ignition on the floor where he couldn't see it or take the key. I gave him a twenty and tried to talk some sense into his head. It didn't sink in at first, but eventually he got out and joined a band of street thugs who laughed at his story.

Strike two for me, I guess.

At a gay bar in Manhattan called the Anvil, there seemed to be a murder every night. Oh, but wait! Murder is she-she and chic.

Huh? That's the kind of gay crap I never got. It's okay to murder each other if your lover is cheating on you? Or because someone got in your way to some guy? Nuts!

I think some gays act like they accept violence and murder because it makes them look tough.

I had an employee who kept insisting that I read books written by serial killers, as if I would learn something from the gory details of how they slaughtered innocent strangers. I believe that many young men pretend to idolize serial killers so they are not challenged to fights.

The fact is, most of them would brown their underwear if they ever were in Vietnam with me and other manly guys of all sexual orientations. There were lots of us in the service, but we were men, not Halloween costume queens or leather and tattoo queens or the ones who wear cowboy hats, construction helmets, and chaps.

I do have one funny story related to this topic. It concerns my dear friend and super fag hag Gina, an Italian immigrant from Sicily. Gina was a middle-aged woman with children who sold cocaine in gay bars. I always got a big kick out of her because Gina's looks and mannerisms reminded me of a younger version of my own Grandma Saporito.

One day while watching TV, Gina heard about a serial killer for the first time. When her children came home, she warned them never to eat breakfast cereal again. When they asked why, Gina blurted out, in mixed Italian and English, "Because there's a cereal killer poisoning all the Cheerios!" Well, that was a laugh in our crowd for many years.

Gina, by the way, had a very handsome young son. Although he was twenty years old and gorgeous, we didn't dare approach him out of respect for Gina.

Violence against gays has been the norm among some straight males and even some of their female partners. It's been common for them to go out in groups to meet gay men and beat on them or worse.

I have a friend named Robert who likes older men and goes to truck rest areas trying to meet them. One night when he was walking around, a driver lured Robert over to his truck, pulled out a pistol, and aimed it at Robert, who began to run. He then shot Robert, who didn't even know he was wounded until his friend noticed the blood. The shooter had a female in the passenger seat who was laughing like crazy and ripping off her clothes, as if to give her man a reward for shooting the dirty faggot. They didn't even attempt to run but just sat there and had sex and waved in delight, showing off their biggest Romper Room smiles as Robert's friend rushed him to the hospital.

Robert survived but only from sheer luck. The bullet didn't hit any vital organs and passed right through his body. The police shrugged it off, knowing why Robert was at the truck stop in the first place and taking the easy way out for themselves.

I lost a very close friend, Anthony S., to violence. He was a wonderful interior designer and a gentle soul. He was good at what he did, but like most people I knew in the arts, he had no business sense whatsoever. Unfortunately, some young man he had been seeing murdered Anthony some years later at his home in the Ironbound section (and got away with it—what a surprise). Anthony had a habit of getting involved with straight young men, which I made the mistake of doing in later years. But that's another story.

The night Anthony died, he left a message on my answering machine. I returned the call when I got home, not having seen him in a year or so because Anthony was involved in a legal action related to minor drug dealing that ruined his career, even though he was innocent. But when did that ever matter?

Anthony was the director of cultural affairs for Essex County, and the county executive who appointed him dropped him like a hot coal when the charges came out. We always thought the county exec was a closet homosexual, because I remember him way back in the '60s hanging with the Tony Imperiale crew, and every other word out of his mouth was "fag" and "queer," a clear signal that he was hiding something.

Anthony suggested we meet at a local diner called Willie's. We laughed and joked about the days I had my bar in Newark called the Cactus Club, how popular it was then, and all the people we knew from those days. I think I was the last of Anthony's friends to see him alive and well.

That night he was murdered by his Brazilian boyfriend. The boyfriend hit Anthony over the head, took his wallet, and tried to drive away in his car. When Anthony got up and tried to open the driver's door, the Brazilian guy backed up in the narrow driveway, crushing Anthony against a wall.

I went to court to testify against him, and he had the whole Brazilian community from Newark in court every day, staring me down and trying to follow me into the elevator to terrorize me into not testifying. It didn't do anything but make me even angrier and determined to get him convicted.

They had found a copy of a poem I had written on Anthony's body. It was about la la land and how most guys, including us, live there when it comes to sex. It went like this:

> *I used to live in la la land when I was very young*
> *And then I met this gorgeous man, so big and hot and hung*
> *He tore my dress and slapped my face and tossed me on the floor*
> *He pulled my hair and threw me out and pushed me through the door*
> *I miss those days, those la la ways, when I was just a girl*
> *'Cause living life au la la [high-pitched voice here] was best in all the world*

So if you leave your la la land for someone young and hot
Remember you'll return some day, it's all we've really got

The Brazilian guy had a nasty lawyer who used the poem in court, trying to prove that Anthony was into rough sex and liked to get beat up, which possibly led to his death. I had written the poem, not Anthony, but the jury didn't believe me. And as is all too common in hate crimes affecting gay people, the criminal went free and got rewarded, and the victim was buried without even an apology. (Oh well, just another crazy fag who got what he deserved!)

I started calling *The Newark Star-Ledger* the Star Liar because of a scathing article they wrote about me. The paper didn't like me because I was a Republican from the Imperiale crew. Their nasty-assed reporter Robert Braun wrote: "Coincidently, Dan Russo was the last person known to be with Anthony S. alive," among many other vicious lies. He implied that I might have had something to do with Anthony's death. It really upset me to read his words.

The courts were extremely homophobic then and actually stayed that way through the 1980s.
All a gay basher or murderer would have to say was that the victim came on to him, and the judge would either give him a ridiculously light sentence or let him go free. Anthony's murderer became so popular in his native country for beating the American justice system that he wrote a fucking book (probably titled *How to Get Away with Murdering a Good Person in America*) and then did an underwear ad in that lawless country of his. I also heard he was elected mayor of his jerk-off town in Brazil.

I remember finding my friend Michelle crying in the church at Anthony's funeral. I said to her that it should rain because it was such a sad day, and a few seconds later the sky opened up. Then we started to cry together, because it seemed that Anthony was sending us a message.

Chapter 13:
Businessman

Another thing that angers me is the way some straight people consider me a weak businessman because of my sexuality. Throughout my life I've had to keep proving that I'm tough and strong and smart enough. What the hell does my sexuality have to do with my business sense and guts?

Others have come to me acting like they're the "connected" ones and that I should pay them homage or protection or whatever else they want to blow, like hot air, out of their stupid mouths. So I say a few incantations, mention a few words, and throw a few names at them—and *poof!* They seem to disappear like the bad witch in *The Wizard of Oz*, when Dorothy threw water on her.

Unfortunately, I have to admit that my father's family had much more intelligence and business savvy than my mother's side. My father's side, if you recall, was in the bar business for many years, but Mom's family always thought there was some sort of magic or luck involved in running a successful business. It was sad for me to see that. When I tried to tell them otherwise, they wouldn't listen because they were scared of knowledge, or at least that's what it seemed like to me, kind of like many people today over a certain age are afraid of computers.

Mom used to say we have no luck, and I used to answer her by saying you make your own luck in this world, as I feel I have done throughout my life. It took me until I was in my mid-fifties to succeed, but I did because I have this built-in program that doesn't allow me to give up. No matter how much I complain and say I'm going to give up, I never do.

I began working as a bouncer at Charlie's West in East Orange, New Jersey, and at Feathers in River Edge. These clubs were part of the disco dance club scene. Before they opened, there were only places like Penelope's in East Orange, where you took your life in your hands because the gay bars were located in the worst neighborhoods. Charlie's West wasn't any better, and when you left the club, you were on your own.

Although starting off as a bouncer might not seem like a proper education to own your own business, it helped me learn and understand the real workings of a club, its owners and managers, its staff, and most importantly, its customers.

My first management job was at Doop's, an old defunct high-line department store from East Orange's heyday. It had a wonderful layout, with a wrought iron spiral staircase.

My dear friend Anthony helped me with the design and decorating work. I remember the first Christmas. I brought dozens of different-sized trees, and we grouped them in different corners of the club, with elegant department store boxes tied with fancy ribbons under every tree.

The owner, Joe Lonzello, became my friend and taught me more about the bar business than I could ever learn anywhere else. Joe was also an avid gambler and blackjack player and taught me that as well.

After working as a bouncer and managing a gay bar called Tory's in the Chelsea section of New York City in the early 1980s, I opened my first gay bar, the Cactus Club, in the Ironbound section of Newark in

1983. My mother asked about the clientele, and when I told her it was gay, she replied in her typical kind manner, "Well, it's a shame. They need somewhere to go too, huh, Bobby?"

Being in the gay bar business taught me many lessons, but the biggest one was to stay in the straight bar business because the gay crowd is small and fickle. Through the years in the bar business, I always was considered the bad boy and got blamed for anything that happened in any of my competitors' clubs. If a light bulb burned out, it was Dan Russo's doing.

When I tried to open Fraternity, a gay bar in Fairview, New Jersey, I got so much trouble from the town and its ignorant mayor that it was hardly worth it. The mayor thought Satan was moving in. I sought support from gay rights organizations but got nothing besides hot air. So my lawyer friend Richard Gruber got the town to back off. The courts were a lot more progressive than the local politicians back in the mid-1980s. The news media was also very supportive, which I appreciated, but the gay community was not helpful at all.

I was painted as the bad guy. The talk went something like this: "Oh, it's just that crazy Dan Russo again. He's trying to hurt Feathers by opening a bar in Bergen County."

Yeah, right. The reality of it was much more about business. The assistant manager of Feathers, Joe Passapia, told me the club was closing and the crowd needed somewhere else to go. But as it turned out, they didn't close because the straight owner was a pig and wanted too much for the building. When construction for a new business and office complex began, they built it around Feathers. So when Feathers didn't go out of business, my club was seen as competition.

The owner of Feathers even tried to tie me to a minor fire he started for insurance claims, but that didn't work. As the fire raged, the staff and drag queens managed to get some receipts with my club's name, Fraternity, and scatter them around the entrance so the fire inspector would find them. I asked the inspector if he thought I set the fire.

"Oh yeah," I said to him, before he could answer, "here is how it went. I set the fire in Feathers. Then, in a wild frenzy, I did a fertility dance in the doorway, threw my arms in the air, and released the club receipts, shouting *woo hooo!*"

The fire inspector just laughed.

Feathers was owned by a straight guy who didn't like gays at all but who sure liked their money. He had his gay employees tell the customers that they were the owners, and he had talentless, lip-syncing drag queens doing shows there. One year in the heat of the summer I decided to do an AIDS benefit at my club Fraternity and had many top recording artists of the time do the benefit for free. The Featherettes, as they called themselves, did their usual PR job on me and told the crowd through their bartenders and drag queens that I was using the AIDS benefit to compete with their ten-year anniversary.

The fact is, Feathers never had their anniversary party in the summer. No matter. The crowd believed them. Although I gave all the night's receipts to AIDS research, we had a half-assed crowd. Meanwhile, Feathers was jammed. It was a shock that they would hold their anniversary party on the same night as my AIDS benefit to make me look bad. It hurts me to this day that they had no respect for what we were trying to do, but I guess when a straight homophobe owns a gay bar, that's what happens. Some of the crowd saw the truth and were disgusted by the actions of the Featherettes, since they remembered going to past anniversaries in the cold months wearing coats.

In the meantime, Charlie's West, whose owners stole the name from a popular New York gay club chain called Uncle Charlie's, was the biggest cocaine store of all. Tommy, the bigger asshole of the two owners, was a nasty cokehead and drunk who sold drugs and pushed drinks to anyone, no matter how plastered they were.

Tommy drove up Route 280 blazed out of his mind nightly. For many years, the New Jersey State Police investigated him for a hit and run by his exit, but they never could prove it. His partner Larry was a big phony and a cokehead in his own right. They had no interest in the safety of their customers. Sad to say, Larry later committed suicide after he was diagnosed with AIDS.

If you were interested in someone and they were too, they'd start talking to the guy right in front of you. If that didn't work, Tommy and Larry had one of their cokehead friends approach him, invite him to a party, and promise cocaine. That's something I never did in my clubs.

Most gay clubs in my observation were nothing more than drugstores, with their own security and bartenders selling the product. I never allowed that to go on in my clubs. Even my friends who sold their wares knew not to do it in my clubs, because if I caught them I would have turned in their asses like anyone else. Most other bar owners and managers thought I was a fool, but I didn't like the drug crowd and the liabilities of allowing that.

Of course, I started getting into the drug scene for a while. I was lured by the glamour of it, but I never sold it in my clubs and I didn't do it that much. Although when Fraternity burned down, everyone said the old line that it all went up my nose. In fact, it had nothing to do with drugs. It was an unfortunate fire that I had no control over, and I had no insurance either.

I was really disliked by many gays who were into the bar scene, but those who liked me were better people by a long shot. I was glad the creepy druggie types didn't like me and avoided my clubs.

I never ran a whorehouse or a drug store. If you wanted to buy drugs or get laid, you needed to go to other clubs, because I wasn't a drug dealer or a pimp. And it brought a better class of customers, employees, and male and female dancers to all my clubs.

The early to mid-1980s were great times for me because I had the opportunity to open and operate the Cactus Club in the Ironbound section of Newark. It was a very unusual and popular club where you could dance to the songs the DJ would spin or sit at the bar and enjoy the male dancers who were right in your face on the bar.

The Cactus Club idea was one whose time had come—a go-go bar for gays to see hot young male bodies dancing, just like the straight bars had done and succeeded at for many years before. There had never been a club like it before in the metropolitan New York area, and it was an instant hit.

The people who came to the Cactus were from all walks of life, and I even had some reunions with old friends from the Waldorf and Penn Station. Also, there was a huge gay population that had moved to Newark's Forest Hill section, buying up those grand old mansions and renovating them to the nines.

The other clubs were upset because it had never been done the way we did it in the Cactus Club. In the other clubs, they would always have some silly, lip-syncing drag queen turn off the dance music and clear the dance floor, who would then announce, in a raspy, annoying, whiny voice, "Show time! Show time!" After lip-syncing a popular song to a record, "she" would announce the male dancers one at a time.

"Oh, this is Tony, and he has a big one . . ." (yeah right, and I'm the tooth fairy.) " . . . and he likes big, muscular guys. But he would consider a little guy if you're well-hung."

In the meantime, the poor dancer is actually straight and can't wait to get out of the club for fear of a hundred fags attacking him for his imaginary huge tool. Or some young dancer barely eighteen would be introduced as an up and coming triple-x porn star who, of course, was very well endowed and wanted to practice on older guys in the crowd. Nothing could have been further from the truth, and the guy, even if he was gay, would have this look of terror on his face. The whole thing was boring and upset the mood of the party.

So I did it my way at the Cactus Club. It worked much better to keep the dance floor and the music going, with male dancers constantly on the bar for those who wanted to watch them.

The place became a legend, and men from all over the world would stop there whenever they flew into Newark International Airport on business. Cheap drinks, a low cover charge, plus hot young men on the bar? That was a big draw back then.

I made sure my bar staff was friendly and hot, since that was also a huge draw in any bar. Besides that, it was nice for my newfound friends and me to be around fun people. In fact, the crowd became a group of friends unto themselves, and after a while we started to hang out together on days when the club was closed.

I couldn't believe how popular I was because of that club. I became an instant local celebrity and got invited to lots of functions and parties. The club was even well known in New York City, and I was invited to parties there as well. I was amazed and delighted by the popularity the Cactus Club had in all of these circles.

At one point, some of our Italo/American guys formed a cummara club on my suggestion. It was so much fun to use it as a reason for special events, like receiving a real Papal blessing from the Pope through our own Cummara Sal.

But gays get bored very quickly, and soon the Cactus Club became "tired" and "so last year." I tried to keep interest going but to no avail. It seemed it was time to move on, so I attempted to open Fraternity, a new and larger club. This was a total disaster for me, a complete failure, and the club eventually burned down without insurance.

Of course, the drag queen community from Feathers said the Mafia and I planned the fire and that I collected a huge insurance claim. But in reality, the fire started in another store in the strip mall where Fraternity was located, and the whole mall went up in flames. I lost everything.

I had my own drag queens at fraternity but the two of them where good guys. Phil Marino aka Miss Mess whom i named one night and it stuck . . . And kevin jackson who was Diana Ross's twin where funny and very entertaining and stuck with me when we did our aids benefit and shows. Real people.

In 1995 I opened a straight, all-nude juice bar in Union, known as Hott 22. The town gave me hell, arrested me illegally, and gave me huge fines when the deal my lawyer struck with them called for a very lenient fine and no jail.

My attorney and friend Ira Weiner called my entire family, and they all refused to put up their houses if I needed bail. My friend and former employee from years ago, Maurice McCoy, offered to put his home up. He was a good guy who also happened to be a black guy.

I had thoughts of revenge for years after the town did that to me, but I never did anything except keep trying to win in the upper court system.

I sold Hott 22 in the last year or so. It's still clean and run strictly by the laws and constitution of the state of New Jersey, despite what local politicians want to say about it. They charged me with the RICO (racketeer influenced criminal organization) act and other lies just to harass me and hurt my reputation. What really pisses me off is that one of the local dum dum politicos responsible for those RICO charges had a father who was a legendary local mobster notorious for terrorizing local doctors and dentists out of their money. So now his son is an elected official in the same town. Well, that figures.

Of course, most of the unsavory individuals I know will tell anyone who will listen that I got ahead by screwing everybody. They think that's the only way you can get a leg up in this world. My own sister said that about me when Fraternity burned down without insurance. So I asked her, "Why am I struggling to pay my bills if I have all that money I screwed everyone out of?"

One guy in jail was talking to a friend of mine who happened to be visiting another inmate. This guy said the same crap—about how I got ahead by screwing everybody—but what was he in jail for? Writing lots of bad checks for thousands of dollars to friends and local merchants.

Sometimes I think about human nature and what makes some people have a deep and burning need to make everyone else look bad so they can look good. As Mom would say, "They wipe the mud off of their faces and rub it on yours."

Another major reason why people are petty is that if you succeed and they don't, which is usually the case, you make them look like failures in life. So it's easy for them to denigrate your success by saying you screwed people.

Don (a.k.a. Eleanor Roosevelt) once told me something I would never have considered if he hadn't mentioned it. We were talking about how I had finally found a business, Hott 22, that was successful and worked well for a decent length of time. Don told me I should be grateful for my success, because of all the people we both knew, I was the only one who succeeded in life. Maybe that's why some people stopped talking to me when I started making serious money.

Lots of people and especially local politicians still think I have big mob connections in New York City. Despite their attacks and frivolous legal actions, I've more than made something of myself, and they can't believe that. It's the same as saying, "Oh yeah, Dan Russo, I know him. He screwed everybody around him to get where he is in business."

Right!

Chapter 14:
A Walk on the Wild Side

My mom always said I had a *"facia di putanna,"* or "the face of a whore," so here goes. Do you know what the most intense, exciting fantasy is for most men and many women?

It's the fantasy of your mate or ex-mate doing something very down and dirty with someone else, especially if you don't like the person they're doing it with. I call it "jealous horns," and it's been my route to multiple orgasms in the same day.

Try it. Picture the love of your life, whether you're still together or apart. He/she is doing some dirty street thugs, letting them sexually abuse his/her body, and he/she loves it. You try to stop the thugs, but your love pushes you away and doesn't let you touch him/her. But the thugs are having their way with your love's body. Believe it or not, this fantasy has cured my erectile dysfunction.

The flip side of this coin is that Hank, my most recent ex, actually did this in some sleazy whorehouse in the Ironbound section of Newark. He told me about their huge members and how they rammed him so hard he came about three times in a row. At first I hated Hank and threw him out, but then I saw a video that could have been him on X Tube and, oh boy, I went into jealous orbit. That was how I wound up fantasizing about it.

But please understand, I realize that the fantasy is better than the reality, and if I actually saw Hank doing it that way, I probably would have lost my lunch and left.

Although Hank was a gorgeous man, he was also a real pig and would do anything with anyone, and I mean anyone—black, white, yellow, mixed, male, female, young, old, fat, skinny, dirty, clean, or whatever—just for the fun of it. And from what I've seen, he's done all that and more.

But fantasy will always be a part of sex. I've had my own real-life fantasies come true, as I hope we all have.

A real eye-opener for me was the 1965 New York City blackout. At the time I had a friend named Al, who we called Big Alice because of his large frame and height.

The generator they had in New York City was called Big Allis, after the company that built it, Allis Chalmers. So when all the New York newspaper headlines read "Big Allis Down Again" or "Down Goes Big Allis," we all jumped at the chance to mail those headlines to our own Big Alice, insinuating he was down on yet another man. He was so good about it and laughed it off.

The New York Times surprised us by saying that the police had to keep chasing the city's "odd people" (meaning gays) from the dark, unlit corners of closed stores, where they were taking advantage of the blackout and having sex.

The truth is, many of us were sorry we missed out on the action. Anonymous sex was and is a great fantasy and the main drive for so many gay and bi men, although many want to paint a rosier picture of the so-called "gay lifestyle."

In my opinion, it isn't a lifestyle at all. For many it's simply something they do in bed that's different than the norm, and for a few minutes a week at that.

Once I had a bar in Clifton called Jump. This young rough man (who was so brutally handsome women would faint) found out where I was and came in there wearing a hot, three-piece Canalli suit. He grabbed my crotch and said loud enough for every gay guy at the bar to hear, "Do you still have that big Italian dick?"

"Well, where could it have gone without me?" I replied. We went outside to find his girlfriend in his car. I followed them home, and she waved good-bye to us. Then we went to my house and I drilled him like crazy. He was a true wild child, but what a cokehead. He kept snorting and wanting more sex, until he finally passed out. Years later he called me from jail and tried to scam me, but I knew the game and told him so.

When it came to acting out your wildest urges, the so-called backroom bars of the '60s and '70s were a big draw. The songs seemed to match the action. For instance, "Gimmie Dat Thang" was playing as guys slipped through the throngs of men, groping for everyone they had an interest in. If they found the right package, down their head would go for one or more man at a time, and maybe even a back door man. But what bothered me is they didn't even know who was backdooring them. They actually found that to be part of the fun, like they did at the St. Mark's baths or in the trucks by the river.

Rock Hudson was known to be gay for many years before he contracted AIDS and brought it to the whole world's attention. Rock was also known to go to a backroom bar in Manhattan known as The Strap, where he'd bend over the pinball machine and let guys line up to take turns.

Unfortunately, these same places became body odor factories because some gays, in their wisdom, decided you needed a little manly smell to be allowed into their respective bars. If you dressed neat (which was anything but dirty jeans and a scruffy tee shirt) and smelled of cologne, you were told to go home and roll around in the mud before you came back.

One night at The Anvil or some other dump, they were celebrating the birthday of the Marquis de Sade. As the crowd roared with glee, a huge black bodybuilder fisted a small blond boy, who looked like he was stoned out of his mind. This caused the young, frail boy to faint. I was disgusted and left with a sick feeling, thinking about this poor lad and his family and what his future would be. It took months for me to stop thinking about it.

Until AIDS showed up on the scene, these wild backroom sex bars thrived in New York City. Guys from all over the world would have anonymous sex in threesomes and foursomes. The worst part is that they didn't even know who they were having sex with, nor did they care.

I never liked the kinky side of sex, straight or gay, and was an outcast in some gay circles for that reason. There were circle jerks (jo's in a circle) and orgies and Mazola oil parties, where everyone would strip down and wallow around together in the substance, while sucking and fucking each other for days with their drugs of choice and lots of booze. The drug culture seemed to leach into the gay community sooner and much easier than it did in the straight one because of the whole underground side to it.

You could find every fantasy you wanted in downtown Newark in the early to mid-60s, from drag queen sex, to a stud like Big Bobby, to S&M sex and more. This was before the straight world knew of such practices. The first I ever heard of the straight world practicing S&M and bondage and discipline was when they raided a home on Clifton Avenue in Newark, arrested Monique von Cleef for running an S&M operation, and deported her back to her native Holland for sordid sex acts.

The county sheriff who I mention in this book was among those on von Cleef's list. He was a true fiend with an insatiable appetite for both money and young people of either sex.

But fantasy will always be tied up with sex (no pun intended). My friend Don (Eleanor Roosevelt) had many funny stories about how he had to role play with other men. He had this mid-thirties guy come over once a week wearing a three-piece suit and sporting a nine-inch, fat tool. The guy made Eleanor wear a red pigtail wig and keep repeating, as he was going down on the guy, "No, no, no, Uncle Georgie (pause). I won't tell my mommy (pause). Don't let me suck your dick (pause, pause, pause) again!"

And the guy would say, "Shut up, Wendy, you little slut. Keep doing it—and get your little girlfriends to do it, too."

I guess that was better than the guy acting out the fantasy with a real-life Wendy.

Chapter 15:
The Mob

The Newark wise guys had their own meaning of "whacked," which was a helluva lot different from the way we used the word. The whole wise guy thing went on all around us, and most people were as oblivious to the mob scene as they were to ours. But I knew them. Growing up in the same Italian neighborhood, how could I not? Not knowing my sexuality, they respected me, because I knew how to mind my business and keep my mouth shut.

Lots of guys thought that some of my close friends and I were Mafia. They talked about it among themselves but never to us.

The fact is, my brother Crazy Joe was somewhat connected, as they say, and when this two-dollar lobster mobster named Lou Cash found out Joe was my brother, he had a question for me.

"Hey, Danny Russo, how come you aren't a big, tough wise guy like your brother Joe?"

And my answer was a classic one: "Let me tell you something there, Lou Cash. You ought to be glad I'm not like my brother Crazy Joe. You get what I mean here?" And old Lou Cash just put his head down.

Brother Joe had an annoying habit of calling everyone I introduced him to a jerkoff. So one day I said, "Everybody is a jerkoff to you, huh?"

His answer was typical of Joe. "Well, everyone but me and some of my friends." So I guess he had some jerkoffs for friends.

Brother Joe had his own mob spin after collecting a vig on a small loan he made to me for two years. He told my sister in the style of Michael Corleone that he would murder me for his money, but only after Mama died. I could hear *The Godfather* theme playing as she told me. As only karma and God would have it, Joe died years before Mom.

This whole Mafia thing is a bunch of crap perpetrated by the FBI and J. Edgar Homo, another self-hating gay who had a male roommate for most of his adult life and liked to cross-dress.

Isn't there a corrupt network on Wall Street and among the big corporations? Well, this whole Cosa Nostra thing is the Italian/American version, you see. But the "others" don't like the fact that it's a strong force to be dealt with. So they brand successful Italian Americans as "mob connected." The Jews were involved in the same style of big business as well, but they saw the light by the middle of the twentieth century and got themselves conventional educations so they could join the ranks of corporate America. A lot of Italians didn't take that route.

Anyone who thinks that corporate America doesn't have its roots in criminal activity is naïve, as Michael Corleone said in *The Godfather*. In my view, that movie is about the struggle between corporations and so-called organized crime. At any rate, the power brokers don't like people like me because I can always make something happen and have always made money without bowing like some puppet on a string to their every whim.

I see through the political leaders on both sides who will take my money and give me nothing in return. Better yet, these political bastards have tried to give me hell through frivolous and unconstitutional prosecution because of the businesses I've had, with no objections from their arrogant, politically appointed judges. It has cost me a fortune in legal fees, while local taxpayers pay their bills (rewarding legal practices that are the politicians' campaign contributors). This is their version of organized crime—they have judges and politicians in their pockets like so many nickels and dimes, just like the Italian "criminals" do.

The Italian organizations in Newark were mostly the Camorra, a ruthless and cunning group from Naples who knew the ins and outs of law and politics and who still exist in Naples today.
Some distant cousins of mine, Pasquale Carmine and Salvatore Russo, were recently arrested while hiding out at a remote farmhouse outside Naples.

A Camorra member recently tried to get close to me while doing some work at my home. This is how they try to gain your confidence and get your information, especially if they see you're older and alone.

What an incredible web of tricks and lies, trying to get close to me in order to extract money and information about my business. Only this time I was well aware of his antics, having seen them many times before in my youth. So I just played his silly game and waited for the right moment to cut him off. I don't rat anyone out, so I didn't report it to any law enforcement group. I was raised to keep your fucking mouth shut, no matter what. This is a theory that most young people today wouldn't understand. Shortly thereafter he was arrested and deported back to Naples, where he belongs.

Bobby Sarcone was a good man and honest attorney who tried to run for governor of New Jersey as a Republican but was shot down for mob ties, as all Italian-Americans are. Bobby had that great combination of balls and brains that I like to believe I have, and he stood up for the people until the corporate mob got him good. I saw Bobby recently and was surprised he was still around. But he's just a frail old man now.

Then there was Ralph deRose, a Democrat who tried to win the nod for governor. But corporate mob USA didn't consider him a real threat, so they let him run and lose.

We in the Italian American community were all for both Italian-American candidates, although they were on opposite ends of the political spectrum. It was an eye opener for me to see how a few insiders control elections. It's the same with the stock market, which is the biggest scam ever to be committed against the average person.

The Mafia is strictly Sicilian, but of all the top Italian crime organizations, namely Puglia's Sacro Croce, Calabria's N'dragnada, and Sicily's Mafia, the Camorra of Naples is considered to be the most ruthless, clever, and secretive. It's the Camorra that corporate America fears more than the Mafia because of their stealth and cunning. Go ahead, Google Camorra and see what you get—next to nothing. I give them a lot of credit for that fact.

Mayor LaGuardia of New York City dealt with these Italian organizations in a most ingenious and unexpected way. LaGuardia, a.k.a. the Little Flower, was bought and owned by corporate America, and being Italian himself, he knew the danger posed by these organized families to his comfortable little world. So in a move that mirrored how other cities controlled blacks and minorities, Fiorello the traitor cut the Italian immigrant section off from the rest of Manhattan by creating Houston Street (pronounced how-ston, for all you non-New York people) and an extension of Seventh Avenue. But you'll never hear that history on TV. You see, it looked good for an Italian to screw other Italians in the name of the law and decency. Ha, ha, ha!

Just as America chopped up our beautiful Italian names, they also chopped up our neighborhoods and organizations.

The Italian and Jewish political leaders in Newark also took actions to benefit themselves and line their pockets under the excuse that they were keeping the Mafia from spreading. I was born and raised in the old Bianchi building in Newark's Little Italy of Seventh Avenue and Cutler Street. What a shame that the politicians tore up that section by building numerous low-income housing projects, naming them (of course) the Columbus Homes.

The Columbus Homes! A stroke of genius, they must have thought, and within five years they became infested with drugs and crime, destroying the old neighborhoods. What scum these politicians were, to destroy a wonderful Italian neighborhood that could still be thriving today, like Bensonhurst in Brooklyn, New York. The roots were so deep in Newark's Little Italy that it still took forty to fifty years to destroy it completely.

To show you how the system worked, the local politicians distributed bus tickets and food vouchers to blacks and other minorities in southern states so they would move into the Columbus Homes, thus securing themselves a huge voter block for the next election. These politicians are all dead now, and I'm sure hell has a special place for them and the rest of the world's self-servers.

Congress is now considering counting illegal immigrants in the latest census. Why? Well, it's simple. If they count all or most of the illegal population, there will be more liberal districts and they will have more liberal congress members, simply because where there are poor people, there are liberal voters, and illegal immigrants always live in those areas.

Getting back to my mob memories, my Grandpa Saporito used to hang at Gabriel's Tavern on Seventh Avenue in Newark, where he was friendly with Sinatra's godfather, Richie "The Boot."
One day during Prohibition, Richie gave Grandpa a new Cadillac and loaded it up with booze. Poor Grandpa got stopped by the cops, who confiscated the liquor and the Cadillac and made him walk home. That was the end of his Mafia career.

I felt constantly haunted whenever people said I had big Mafia connections and then tried to set me up for a fat loan they had no intention of repaying. This happened with a friend who always expressed his belief in honesty and valor got a rather large loan from me and never repaid a dime. Yet, when I owed him money once, he constantly reminded me of the loan and asked for the money.

I guess my "mob connections" didn't scare him, and my friendship wasn't worth the money. Granted, this was a guy who gave me a loan of $1,500 when I desperately needed it, but I would have thought he would pay me back as I paid him. This guy was what we call a "leather queen," and I could never go through life with all that leather and all those tattoos. How in hells bells do you think you can fit into society dressing and acting like that? I don't think these leather queens can see themselves as they really are. They expect everyone to respect and accept them as normal. Huh? Another aspect of gay life I can't understand.

The worst part of the loan was that shortly after I gave him the money he so desperately needed, he started spending thousands of dollars on buying these fucking parrots. So I guess he desperately needed parrots? Maybe they were having a Freda the Bird Woman look-alike contest, and the grand prize was a house and car made entirely of leather.

There are only a few old friends I have known for years and still consider friends, such as Paul, a.k.a. Rose V., because he looks and acts like his mother of the same name. We've been through a lot of hard times and are still friendly, although our life choices keep us from seeing each other more than a few times a year. Even so, we had a major business loss together and it didn't harm our friendship. Paul was also my business partner at the Cactus Club in Newark.

The fact is, all the real mobsters are either dead, retired, or in prison. Although there are a few exceptions, most of what's left are make-believe mobsters, or what I like to call "lobster mobsters"—those who either inherited their power from family or because nobody else wanted to be in that position these days with the FBI coming down on them.

There's a third type that isn't "connected" at all, like the ladies' shoe salesman who terrorized my managers and security for months until I ran into him at my club one day. As my little pussy manager sat on the ledge outside my club wiping sweat off his face from fear, I stood there toe-to-toe with this lobster mobster, who was trying to scare me with all of his bullshit lines and made-for-TV moves. So I finally asked him if he knew a few people I knew, and he ran off into the night, never to be seen or heard from again.

Speaking of mob, real and lobster, let's face it, President John F. Kennedy was murdered by the mob as payback for his father's mistake of promising the mob an ear to the White House if they helped rob the 1960 election in Chicago and other cities for his son. JFK won by less than a tenth of a percentage point nationally and by a few thousand votes in Illinois. The Kennedys stole the election, as they had in many other American elections, and then Bobby Kennedy came down on the mob hard, going as far as dropping one mobster off in the jungles of some obscure country like Guata-la-bing-bang without any means of getting home. Well, the mobster returned and got Oswald to kill Bobby's brother, because, in the words of the mobster, if you cut off the head, the rest of the snake dies along with it. I'm not someone in the know. It's just that the story makes perfect sense.

Don't get me wrong, I never much liked the Kennedys and their "let the sunshine in" brand of politics, but you don't kill the president and expect this country to shake it off like you've just killed Joey Falafondosh in his Lincoln Town Car. How awful that assassination was. How bad for America, and how much it changed us.

But just remember—Joe Kennedy and the mob stole that election from Nixon, so if it had gone the honest way, which usually doesn't happen in the big cities, Kennedy would have not been president and therefore not been killed.

I was in boot camp in the navy when they announced that the president had been assassinated. Because we had no outside communication, we found out three days after it had happened. It put a chill up my spine worse than the wind at the Great Lakes boot camp had. It happened on November 22 and we found out three days later, November 25, which happened to be my birthday. How sad.

We thought that Russia did it, or maybe Castro, and we were sure we were going to war soon. The whole Kennedy thing was why the FBI finally had it with the American Mafia. Bobby Kennedy got it the same way, because the mob knew if he won the presidency he would continue his fight against them in a vendetta for his brother's murder. I believe he was trying to clean up this country, and it was a real shame how they murdered them. Joe Kennedy should have coached his son in diplomacy, and actually Bobby should have known better, but he, like most American youth with any kind of family money, was sheltered from reality. It's the same thing when kids today hang out in the hood with the brothas, get their heads bashed in with a bottle, excuse it away as an isolated incident, and then go back for more. How sad for the Kennedys, and how sad for America's young people.

A last mob memory involves Charlie Casagrande, my good friend and a good guy. Choo Choo Charlie, as we called him, was a handsome Italian-Irish young man who loved being a tough guy. He always won his fights and never backed down from one. But like me, Charlie also had a good heart.

I started hearing stories about Charlie being involved in the mob, and I was disappointed in him, because I never knew him to be an outlaw or mobster, and my knowledge of that period's wise guys was pretty good.

One night I was at Penn Station in Newark when a mutual friend drove up to the curb. I won't mention this friend's name because he's still alive as I write this book, but the friend was in a panic, telling me that Choo Choo was in big trouble and needed my help immediately. So I jumped in this guy's car and off we went to Branch Brook Park, which still is one of the largest urban parks in North America.

When we got to the park, there was Charlie, blood still flowing from his groin and chest, his penis sewn in his mouth with the head sticking out. A knife in his heart looked like it had been twisted Sicilian style, and he had the most horrified expression on his face. I had to ask the friend what was in Charlie's mouth, because I didn't want to believe it.

The cops were already there and told us to leave as I held back tears of anger.

I asked this friend what the hell happened to our buddy, and he said Choo Choo had sex with the wrong guy, an old mobster, and gave him syphilis, which the mobster brought home to his wife.

Poor Choo Choo. He didn't have any STDs, as it turned out. The mobster had gotten it in New York from some filthy street scum he had sex with for ten dollars. Because he was drunk when it happened, the mobster forgot about that partner and only remembered having sex with Charlie. This old idiot later tried to apologize to me for killing my friend, but I told him to fuck off.

There was supposed to be a ghost in Branch Brook Park called "the white lady" that was seen around a certain tree. They had tied Charlie to "the white lady" tree. I wonder if the ghost people saw after that was really poor Charlie's tormented spirit.

Chapter 16:
AIDS, Part 1

I was butch, which in today's words meant I was a top man who didn't ever allow anyone to bend me over. There were hardly any guys like me, except for one who I called Betty Butch because he liked to claim he was straight. But he definitely was not.

I have to sadly say that the reason why I'm still alive today and most of the wonderful characters I've told you about are not is the simple reason that I didn't like it on the bottom and they did. It was the ones on the bottom who got AIDS.

The versatile coupled gays were the saddest of all, because they would give it to each other, and then one would watch the other one suffer a fate that he was also doomed to live out.

I never understood why so many of them had to have a third person for exciting sex, because if they stayed monogamous, they would have stayed healthy. But who in hell am I to judge? And who knew this horrific disease would come?

The big problem with the gay mentality is this unstoppable drive to have sex with every man they see. I was a body builder for most of my youth. Gay friends would ask me to take them to the gym to show them how to work out. The annoying part was when we got to the gym, these guys weren't interested in working out at all.

They stood around like statues, staring at the other men who were there.

They would hit on your current partner, your brother, your employee, or anyone else they saw. I would be driving with a gay friend, and he'd be looking nonstop at every man we passed in a car, truck, bus, on a bike, or walking down the street. Like hungry wolves or vampires, they stare and stare and lose their sense of conscience, blocking out the whole world just to check out some dude's butt or crotch.

I lost my only two true loves, Darren and Stash, to AIDS. They caught it years after we broke up, but it still hurt a lot. They came back to be with me during their last months. What happened was that they got friendly at one point and started to share men and do drugs in New York's seedy leather bars.

So many young gay and bi men went like sheep to the slaughterhouse and quietly accepted their doom. So many of our friends, both young and old, were dying of AIDS at one point that men I didn't much care for would greet me cordially in my gay bars. They'd smile and say, "Well, we made it." And I'd say, "Yeah, well, so far, anyway." And together we'd let out this nervous laugh.

My first loss to AIDS was Bob Wright. Like many older gay and bi friends, and even a few straight ones, he stopped talking to me because I had some money and he didn't. Instead of letting me pay for his coffee and plain Jane burger, he would bring his own Devil Dog or Ring Ding that he hid under a napkin so he wouldn't have to pay for dessert at the local diner. After drinking dozens of cups of coffee because of the bottomless cup policy, he would get all jittery and then ask me to stop at the local CVS pharmacy. I waited for Bob so damn long in the car that I finally had to go inside to see what was taking him. No surprise—he was trying to trick the cashier, saying he gave her a twenty when in fact it was a ten. That was the last time I saw Bob W., who I called Cyclops because of this huge lump on his forehead.

Bob invented a homemade accu-jack masturbating machine from a three-speed Volkswagen bus's windshield wiper unit. He used to keep it in a box in his closet and called it his lover. He explained it one day to a mutual friend, Ward S., who then insisted Bob stop the car so he could get out because he knew Bob had gone crazy.

Bob and I used to frequent the Crescent Diner on Bloomfield Avenue in the Cedar Grove/Verona area, and next door to the diner was an old churchyard. One day we decided to check it out and found one tombstone with mud obscuring the wording. We wiped it away to read the eulogy and boy, were we sorry. I will never forget the inscription.

> *Hark! From the tomb a doleful sound,*
> *My ears attend the cry.*
> *Ye living men come view the ground*
> *Where you must also lie.*

It was the grave of a revolutionary war soldier named David Ogden who died in battle at age twenty. Needless to say, Bob and I never went back. I thought about the tombstone after he died.

Unfortunately, false rumors abounded around AIDS, like getting it from a mosquito or from the air, like Brother Joe once exclaimed on the phone to me. Nobody would listen to me. I felt it was common sense that AIDS was hard to get and that blood and a lack of oxygen were involved.

Joe was the perfect example of a homophobe. When an AIDS patient wound up in Columbus Hospital in Newark in a quarantined room next to our mom, he called me and said I'd better get down there quick, because the door to the room of the AIDS patient was open and
"AIDS was pouring out of the room." I avoided the obvious laugh and tried to explain to big, bad Joe Russo that if you could get AIDS by breathing air we'd all have it, but all he said to me was, "Well, you don't know."

Don't get me wrong. I've had my share of illnesses, such as Hepatitis B in the 70s, all because I wanted to be the brave one and caught a tiny mouse by the tail. Who knew it would twist around and bite my index finger, turning me a pasty yellow within a week?

Then there was Hepatitis C that I'm sure I caught by having sex with someone who had it and didn't care to share his misfortune. And I caught a few other STDs over the years that I won't mention.

I wasn't at high risk, but it broke my heart to watch the deaths of so many of my friends, lovers, and customers.

When I opened the Cactus Club in 1983, all the other bars were using plastic cups and calling them safety glasses, but the real reason was to prevent the spread of AIDS.

I refused to do that and served drinks in regular glassware. When people would ask me, I said I knew you couldn't get AIDS that way. I felt it was the bottom guys who got it.

A few years later that came out to be true, and everyone asked me how I knew so early, like I was CIA or something else. I always got blamed for being a spy or a hit man or some Mafia henchman, but it was all right with me, you see, because power perceived is power achieved.

I met a young man back when I opened the Cactus Club who was of Portuguese descent. He was very handsome, but what a girl he was. Jaime had a natural talent for floral arrangements, and we made sure from opening day we had wonderful flowers every week at the club.

Jaime was enamored with me and made no bones about letting me know it. I followed his lead, and we wound up in a French restaurant in Harrison, New Jersey, of all places, while Edith Piaf sang "t'es beau tu sais," which I decided to translate to Jaime as "you are very handsome." And as Piaf droned out the tune in a sad, tearful, whispering way, Jaime made a scene and stormed out of the restaurant and into the torrential rain of the night, crying his eyes out because I had gone back to Darren and/or some crazy young tomboy female who hung at the club. Jaime was the queen princess of drama queens, as we all knew from the name I gave him—Mona Moss.

After telling Jaime that Darren had AIDS, he exclaimed in a very loud and jovial voice, "Good, he deserves to get AIDS. Should know better!"

As I tried to get him to retract his words, Jaime went on to say, "I'll never get AIDS. I only have safe sex." Then he added with a giggle, "He he, fuck 'em," meaning my Darren, whom Jaime was always jealous of. I told him he was going to pay for those words, but he just waved his girly hand at me and shrugged it off.

I don't know if Jamie is still alive at this point, but I hope he's doing well since he had AIDS the last time I checked with his close friend. After checking obits online, I found none in his name, so that's good.

Chapter 17:
AIDS, Part 2

I had a friend back then we called Peggy Papa who was the cheapest, most paranoid fag I ever met. He owned a beauty salon (of course) called Adorn (tacky and tasteless), and everyone left with really big hair, like they were the cast from Divine's movie *Hairspray*. I'd take my mom there to get her hair done because it was convenient, and he would charge her full price. Peggy also sold clothes that were so old they would tear from dry rot after you wore them once. He'd give you an argument if you tried to bring them back. My poor mom wouldn't complain and would wear them torn and all.

I once ran into Peggy Poo at a gay cruising area. I had just broken up with someone, so I was very depressed. So Peg walked up to me with this "I just saw a ghost" look of fear on his paler-than-usual-face and proceeded to tell me how his partner of many years caught him there just a few minutes ago and tried to run him down with his car.

This gave a big laugh, and I forgot my breakup problems.

But seriously, all I can say for Peggy Poo Poo is that he/she was the queen of big hair for those who couldn't or wouldn't change their styles, and Peggy went down the tubes as the old women who frequented his salon died off.

I was so broke that I would ask him to give me cash on my charge card, and the cheap bastard would charge me 10 percent to do it. Peggy always expected me to pay whenever we were out somewhere and wouldn't even lend me some money when I was away with him and ran short. He was always embarrassing me and acting like the big shot.

What an old lady he was in every way. Peggy even made sure he dated my stupid ex-boyfriend Darryl, who also went out with Judy the Chimp, because then he could shove it in my face, telling me how my ex thought he was the butchest stud he'd ever been with.

I knew better, because Darryl told me Peggy had a skinny little fish hook and got all excited by saying to him, "Who's the boss? Am I the boss?" That gave me a big laugh. There are so many gay dudes who couldn't be butch no matter what but love to be on top and try so hard to put on the man act. The problem is, it never goes over very well.

Peggy Papa wound up meeting some young queen in Branch Brook Park's cruising area, who I knew from the gay bar Charlie's West. I knew he didn't like older men like Peggy Poo and always went after young guys, or as we said, "He was a chicken hawk." I also knew that lots of young fem queens who moved to New York City returned home to Jersey after they got AIDS during the first onslaught of the disease.

So Peggy took the young queen in and had sex with him without protection. The queen then announced that he was sick and needed a place to live out his life, whatever was left of it. Peggy went into orbit, calling me and everyone he knew, saying he was going to die. Every time Peggy Poo would get a cold, she was dying, so I'd say, "What's wrong? Do you have AIDS *again?*"

I finally started calling him Aida.

All his chicken liver friends started avoiding him. When Peggy showed up at one of their queen parties, they served him in paper cups and plates, while everyone else got china. This angered me, because although I knew Peggy Poo wasn't sick except in his own mind, much of the gay community would abandon their friends with AIDS, just as many families abandoned their sons.

There were exceptions, and I take off my hat to those good souls. But too many people didn't support those with AIDS, which was disgusting.

I have never seen so many old ladies come out of their canasta games as when AIDS reared its head in the gay community. There was a pervasive feeling of fear and paranoia that was unacceptable to me. Some old guy who owned a peep show was running around the store with a pail of bleach water, scrubbing down the holes in the walls where guys got some head as they watched porn. I know it sounds disgusting, but men are dogs and need that release, whether you like it or not. Please don't get me wrong here. I'm not saying all men do this, but I would guess some 30 to 40 percent do, yours truly included.

Yes, we are the dogs of humanity, but I've always loved dogs. If we're dogs, at least we're honest about it.

The number and quality of the young men in those booths was super good, because you could meet men who wouldn't go anywhere else and you had total anonymity there. If they got caught, they would say, "Yeah, I go there and drop a few dollars in quarters to get excited by watching porn movies." The owners didn't mind as long as you kept the red light on by constantly feeding the machine. So we paid to get head from some young college student or married dude who wanted revenge on his wife or got what he really needed besides straight Tab A into Slot B sex.

The peep shows were perfect for them. And boy, what hungry little mutts they were when they finally got what they needed.

Being in the bar business around the time AIDS came on the scene, I experienced some sick things. One bastard put the names and addresses of dead AIDS victims on our mailing lists so the dead guys' families would get them. I would then receive sad phone calls and letters from the families asking me to remove their sons' names from our lists. I know hell holds a special place for those who used AIDS for lunatic fringe religious or sadistic reasons.

I loved the lesbians who came out in support of gay men and told those religious fanatic jerkoffs that if God gave AIDS to sinners, he must love lesbians, because they were at least risk to get it. God bless them.

There is a strange love/hate, life-and-death game that goes on in the gay community that I could never accept or understand. I've heard a few stories about HIV positive men asking other men if they could give them the gift that keeps on giving, meaning the AIDS virus. Many gays would write off their sometimes outrageous behavior as chic or "she-she," as they did with the following scenario.

I went to the gay pride celebration day in the early 1980s in New York City, where one anti-Christian protesting stand featured a garbage can filled with urine and crucifixes. That anti-God, anti-Christian attitude was something I couldn't understand about the gay community. I said to my friend Donald (a.k.a. Eleanor Roosevelt) that the gay community would pay for that anti-Christian act. I didn't understand why nobody seemed to get upset by the sight of crosses in a pail of piss.

I objected by screaming and kicking, but nobody seemed to care what I thought. As usual whenever I protested, they would turn their heads and pretend not to hear me. I've experienced this ignorance all my adult life with wild-eyed gay anarchists ignoring me as if I wasn't there, turning their heads and getting busy so I couldn't corner them. But I kept screaming that something horrible would happen to the gay community because of this type of act.

I had no idea how prophetic my words would become when AIDS started destroying the gay community not long after. Sometimes it scares me when things I think actually come to be.

Some men I knew who had lost their partners to AIDS or another opportunistic disease would put on a sad and pitiful act, telling everyone they knew and met that they were strict tops and never got it from their deceased mates. But after a short time they, too, would develop the symptoms and die.

This was before the new meds came on the market that now help many people live with AIDS. I knew this day would come and that I would be upset, because my dear ones who died didn't have those meds. And they weren't the only ones who died, for God only knows how many unsuspecting guys caught it because of their denial.

Men will be men and that's just how it is, but some of the horror stories I know would grow hair on a baby's butt.

I had a dear friend I named Delta Dawn because when caller ID first came out, he started calling me from all the payphones on Broad Street in Bloomfield, asking me what number he had called me from. After the third call, I asked him why he wanted to know all these payphone numbers. His response was comical.

"Well, when I see a cute young guy on one payphone, I go to the next one and call him, asking if he'd like some head." He actually met men that way, so I gave him the name Delta Dawn after the song of the same name, where Delta walks the streets with a suitcase in hand, looking for a mysterious, dark-haired man. What a camp she was, Miss Delta. He eventually died of AIDS and never even told me he was sick.

I later learned he was into some really strange, or shall we say exotic sex, which out of respect for my friend I won't get into, except to say it involved bodily functions. I would never have dreamed that of him if it weren't for another friend who had sex with him. Anyway, Delta was a nice guy, and when I was down and out because of the fire that destroyed my club Fraternity, he was one of the few people who helped me through it with small loans of twenty dollars. And sometimes when I'd ask for twenty dollars, he'd give me fifty dollars.

Damn God-forsaken AIDS took so many of my friends and acquaintances I can't even remember them all. I hear from time to time about a friend from years ago who passed away and it's usually AIDS. I had a few very successful diets during the early days of AIDS, and people would ask me if I was all right, thinking I was sick because I was so thin.

So many good and talented people, and yes, I admit, some not so nice people (but mostly good) were lost to AIDS. And there were so many suicides that it became completely depressing.

There was Ron Maher, who drove his little Honda off a cliff on the Jersey side of the Lincoln Tunnel, and Larry from Charlie's West fame, who took an OD of pills, and Don Jackson, a dentist who killed himself over the horror of his patients wanting to sue him for possibly giving them the virus.

And those are only the ones who offed themselves. There were so many more who didn't want to commit a sin, like my Darren and Stash, who suffered through the pain of diarrhea, nausea, blindness, constant weakness, fevers, and night sweats.

God bless and love them all and forgive any sins. They were all good people for the most part who struggled through what was left of their lives wondering if those lunatic fringe religious bastards were right about God punishing them for being gay. What a shame that supposedly God-fearing people put guilt and fear on those who were about to face a horrible death.

I loved the '60s and '70s because there was no AIDS or AIDS-induced homophobia.

Now there are all these unknown STDs coming out of South America, mostly Brazil, and winding up here. The stories I hear lately from my doctors, one of whom is gay, are really bad. Straight young men are having unprotected sex with other supposedly straight men and spreading these STDs to each other and then to their female partners. So many young American men are checking into hospitals or going to their doctors with nasty symptoms that medical science has no clue about or cure for.

I'm scared and don't think I can deal with anonymous sex anymore. The problem is that we have been taught that everyone is the same and that we are all safe and clean, when the truth is that some of these third-world countries don't know or care if they spread STDs. Here it is again, "Oh yes, I got an STD from that foreign guy or girl, but his/her family was very good to me and helpful about it all. Okay everybody, sing along now. I'd like to teach the world to die in perfect harmony, *la la la la*."

Chapter 18:
A Lost World

In the days before the riots, in fact long before I was born, the old first ward in Newark was a buzzing beehive of Italian-American life.

The multi-story tenements were full of wonderful families, mostly Italian by the time I was born. But there also other ethnic groups—the Irish, Dutch, Polish, German, and Chinese. There were even a few leftover Jews who would tell their sad stories about madman Adolf and show you their concentration camp tattoos. We were all friends and got along very well.

The fruit and vegetable man would shout out the type of veggie or fruit he had that day, and the women would shout back what they wanted. Then the baskets would roll down on pullies with the money and list. He'd fill them with their choices and change, and they would pull it back up, sometimes as high as six stories. I was always fascinated by those baskets and pullies.

We could look out our windows and watch the Saint Gerard feast going on every mid-October. They marched the saint's statue around the neighborhoods, covered with money the people collected for that joyous occasion. The band was comical and belted out old Italian tunes, some of which came from the Mussolini days.

There were zeppole, pizza, sausage sandwiches, torrone candy, and many Italian gifts and recordings. It still goes on today, as it has for more than one hundred years, right around mid-October. It's worth the trip.

The smells from the different sauces were a true delight, and I always sampled them to see what the world tasted like. We never paid attention to the local politicians and their antics. As a result, it was easy for them to eventually destroy the life and world we had forged in Newark's old first ward.

I would run up and down the many flights of stairs and sometimes see things I wasn't ready for at such a young age—young couples having sex in the middle landing, an older dude on a young man, or maybe even two middle-aged women who were cousins. We called them spinsters since they never married and were approaching old age, but I think I know why they never married.

The old Newark of my childhood was a beautiful city. Louie Bamberger of department store fame was responsible for bringing those beautiful cherry blossom trees from Japan to Branch Brook Park, a display said to be even more magnificent than the one in Washington DC.

Many of the judges, politicians, and corporate bigwigs of the time lived in the finer areas of Newark. The Forest Hill section was at the top of that list.

The people who lived in Forest Hill were definitely upper crust. The aristocracy of New Jersey had built their mansions there—the Tiffanys, whose stained glass factory was in Newark, the Bambergers, and opera soprano Madame Maria Jeritza, who made the cover of *Time* magazine on November 12, 1928.

Madame Jeritza's block square compound had numerous houses. I had the opportunity to buy it for $85,000 when she died in the early 1980s, but my friend Anthony, who knew her, said the compound needed major work and talked me out of it.

As it turned out, I should have listened to my heart and not my friend. A gay couple bought Maria Jeritza's complex during the gay gentrification period of the 1980s and after some renovations, sold it for an enormous profit. But I miss and love my dear friend Anthony, and it was only a house.

The highlight of any High Street trip is the great Krueger mansion, the greatest ever built in Newark. It was the home of Gottfried Ephraim Krueger, owner of the Krueger Brewery, Electric Park, and a factor in the local Democratic party. Krueger himself was the son of a farmer from Baden, Germany. He came to Newark in 1853 to work at his uncle's brewery.

Built in 1888 for $250,000 in a style reminiscent of a Bavarian castle, the house has a Louis XIV interior, rosewood floors, stained-glass windows, embossed leather walls, mother of pearl wainscoting, and a five-story atrium capped by an elaborate copper-filigreed dome. The Krueger family moved out after World War I. The mansion was sold to a construction company and then to the Scottish Rite Masons. (New York City Mayor Ed Koch once worked in the coatroom, and I must add that Ed had his own nice closet, although I loved his political candor and brash way of telling people where to go.)

In 1958 the mansion was sold to Louise Scott Roundtree, the owner of a black women's beauty company. Ms. Scott maintained the house very well, but her heirs did not pay property taxes and the city of Newark took over the mansion in 1982.

Sadly, Newark did nothing at all to keep the house up, and it was slowly vandalized beyond recognition. In the late 1980s and early 1990s, Newark, the state, and the federal government spent $7 million to convert the mansion into a black cultural center, but the restoration job proved more difficult than expected. And Newark proved less than up to the job, since the local politicos couldn't extract their cut in the funds.

Mom's extended family lived in Newark and its surrounding towns. They had a habit of staying close by, which was a good thing for us children because there was always a place for us to go. Today you only see that in recent immigrant families.

I remember the Rossi family, who were my mom's cousins. They bought a huge three-story home on a corner right up the hill from us on Third Avenue and Garside Street. What a wonderful family. They always had the coffee pot going and food cooking. They were always playing cards for pennies and nickels around their large dining room table.

The three sisters, Mary, Laura, and Rose, we knew as "the girls." Their mom and dad were my mother's aunt and uncle, and they, like Mom's parents, were the salt of the earth. I bought memorial stones for them and for much of my old family on the grounds of Saint Lucy's Church in Newark, near where they used to live in the early days.

There were so many great restaurants, shops, and bakeries in the old Italian north ward. There were the Versuvius Restaurant and Mama Lucia's and the Seacrest Clam Bar and Biasi's, where my brother Crazy Joe had his wedding, not to forget Nicastro's and the Belmont Tavern, which is still there. It's a big wise guy hang out and as usual for mob hangouts, has great food. In later years Michaelangelo's was owned by a local wise guy whose son was an Elvis lookalike. He'd stand there with his pelvis pushed forward so I could see his monster bulge.

In the Ironbound was Santa Luchia and a little dump with boxes in the windows called Amelia's, with five little old ladies cooking behind the counter and serving the best Italian sandwiches.

There were Italian delis, like Celantano's and the Prosperity Market. Gerruto's had the best handmade Italian sausage. Hobby's Jewish deli in downtown Newark is still there after one hundred years and as good as ever. Ting a Ling's was a great foot-long hot dog place in north Newark, which had the greatest homemade lemon ice with chunks of lemon peel in it.

Dickie Dee's Italian hot dogs is still on Bloomfield and is a Newark phenomenon, serving half a pizza loaf stuffed with one or two hot dogs, onions, peppers, and potatoes, with mustard on the bottom and ketchup on top.

Tony's hot dog truck has been on Park Avenue and Lake Street in north Newark for over forty years, but Tony sold it recently, but its still good.

Broadway Tom's was a pushcart on Broadway in north Newark in the '50s, and it was the best, with hot (spicy) Italian onions and Manhattan special coffee soda.

Giordano's bakery had the best bread, so good Frank Sinatra would fly it to California. I'd walk to the stone-stepped bakery on Seventh Avenue every day for our bread and eat some on the way home. It was hot and fresh, the crust a quarter inch thick and dark brown.i would always talk to the older man behind the counter since we had outed each other when we saw each other at the Waldorf. There were also Dipaolo's and Collandra's bakeries, both of which are still on Bloomfield Avenue. Ferrara's Bakery made the best cakes and pastries. Capri and Ditta Ferreara were good bakeries too, packed on every holiday.

I still get my fresh meats and grated Romano cheese from Violante's Market on Bloomfield Avenue by Grove Street on the Newark/ Bloomfield line.

There were so many good places to eat or to buy special things that are now mostly replaced by fast food joints and convenience markets. What a shame.

The Newark of my youth is long gone, never to return. What brought about its demise were the riots of 1967 and the high-rise, low-income housing projects like the Columbus homes.

Chapter 19:
The Riots

When Newark went up in flames in 1967, we saw it all come down firsthand. In fact, I saw more violence there than I did in Vietnam.

The riots were kindled by out-of-state instigators who went there with a plan to start trouble, burn the black neighborhoods down, and destroy any business that didn't have the words "soul brother" spray-painted on its windows. It reminded me of the photos I saw of Nazi raids on Jewish-owned businesses, how they painted the Star of David on Jewish merchants' windows with the words "Actung Juden!"

It was unfortunate that the downtown merchants were mostly Jews who remembered or certainly knew of the Nazis and had a frightening feeling of deja vu. Unfortunately, they didn't have any words painted on their windows this time around, because "soul brother" would have saved them. It sounds like it was organized to me.

The little Mom and Pop shops were all looted and destroyed. Most of those merchants lost everything and never reopened. Those who tried couldn't get insurance for their businesses or properties.

The looting that went on was unbelievable. I wanted to know what tearing down the area would do for the local poor people. I never figured that one out.

Dick "the Prick" Spina was nowhere to be seen during the violence. I guess he wasn't as brave with rioters as he'd been with gay and bi people at the Waldorf Cafeteria over the years. What an asshole he was with his arrogant ways. He had a lot to do with the lack of police control over the riot. He bragged about his police force when nobody ever saw more than 5 percent of the officers. It was not the officers' fault—they were great, but Spina was a buffoon. Fact is, the police were caught off guard because that old fart of a police commissioner cared more about his hair, his cummara (girlfriend), and his bowtie than the city of Newark and its poor residents of all races. Spina died on top of his long time girlfriend who was a Belleville, New Jersey, commissioner.

Here, based on research and recollection, is what I can tell you about the riots.

Stokely Carmichael, a black man in his mid-twenties, had come to national prominence earlier that year when he helped black candidates overthrow white incumbents in Alabama. Then he began touring the country preaching black power

A flyer passed around the black neighborhoods announced, "Stokely is here" or "Stokely is coming here." Another flyer was being passed around that showed a sketch of our wonderful Bamberger's Department Store with flames shooting out of its windows.

Carmichael's arrival in Newark came as the city was reaching a milestone: for the first time in its history, the population had a black majority. The United Community Corporation (UCC), a federally funded anti-poverty program in Newark, had become a hotbed of activity by African American political activists.

When Carmichael, arrived he told the crowds, "Whether you know it or not, you are the majority in this town. You should already have taken Newark over, because it belongs to you."

Nearly every authority figure in the city was white—from the police, whose reputation for brutality was notorious among the black community, to teachers, to city hall bureaucrats. The mayor, Hugh J. Addonizio, was white and Italian. He appointed blacks to some prominent positions and consulted a council of black ministers he felt represented the African American community's interests.

So as Newark went into the summer of 1967, the unease felt around Springfield and Bergen had a variety of sources. That tension was about to become worse. On Wednesday evening, July 12, 1967, two white Newark policemen arrested a black cabbie, John W. Smith, for improperly passing them.

Differing accounts of what happened next have never fully been resolved. The policemen said Smith resisted arrest and had to be subdued. Smith said the cops started beating him after he asked why they pulled him over. A *Newark Star-Ledger* review of state police archives, along with numerous interviews and an examination of film footage, suggest that Smith's arrest has been overplayed as the spark for the Newark riots.

At any rate, a rumor soon flew around Hayes Homes: the police beat a cabdriver to death.
Before long, protesters were pelting the Fourth Precinct with rocks, the opening melee.

The looting that followed Smith's arrest on the night of the twelfth and morning of the thirteenth, limited to a few stores, was minor compared with what was to come. An emergency command post at the Roseville Armory was activated in case the trouble spread. The lead story in the Newark evening news the afternoon of July 13 was, "Disturbance in central ward called isolated incident." Some merchants escaped the looters' wrath by writing "soul brother" on their store windows, indicating blacks owned them.

There are no exact figures on how many people engaged in looting. Even if it was several thousand, that would be a small percentage of the city's black population, which then was close to two hundred thousand. The majority of residents in the vicinity of Springfield and Bergen remained on the sidelines, horrified by the destruction of their neighborhood.

Still, neither they nor the black community leaders who walked through the area, urging calm, could stop the onslaught.

The Newark police had bigger problems on their hands. Dick the Prick always felt that preparing for a riot only encouraged one, so his officers did not have the equipment or the training for what transpired as darkness fell on July 13. Brilliant, Dickey.

The disturbances in Newark essentially could be split into two events: shopping (by the looters) and shooting (by authorities).

The first phase was a commercial riot, where people broke into stores and took whatever they could carry. The next was a police action that involved lawlessness by some officers. Our National Guardsmen were given explicit instructions to shoot to kill, so you know what that meant.

On Springfield and Bergen streets that Sunday, another problem was pressing on the riot-weary citizenry. All the local food storeowners had closed for fear of bodily harm. UCC, once home to so much idealized revolution, was converted into a relief station.

The six days of rioting and looting left twenty-six people dead and hundreds injured. In my humble opinion, I would multiply the casualties by at least twenty-five. Nobody really knows the right number. Over fifteen hundred people were arrested, and property damage was in the millions.

For me, the song "Soul Finger" by the Bar-Kays was the theme song for the Newark riots, with its sounds of crowds and screaming in the background. It really freaked me out that the song was playing on my radio as I drove down the Garden State Parkway watching Newark burn.

They were handing out guns to people in the north ward, and I got myself a couple. I never had to use them, but it was a comfort to have them. We didn't know what was going to happen, and we had to protect ourselves. But the rioters didn't come up to north Newark. It was an Italian neighborhood, and we would have sent them back in body bags.

All the people that hung downtown sided with the rioters. The mutual admiration and apologies exchanged between black and white gays was so phony it made me nauseous. "Oh, I'm so sorry about what happened to your neighborhood . . ." Many gays thought this was the moment for them to step up and achieve their rights as the blacks had done. They thought they could tie their wagon to the black civil rights struggle.

Nothing could have been further from the truth. Gay rights would be abused and stepped on for over twenty-five more years. Even as I write this book, gays aren't treated in the same way other so-called minorities are, and we'll probably never enjoy the same freedoms that most people do. Even with a president whose father was black, gays don't have the same rights that the rest of America has, and blacks refuse to allow gays to revel in their victories because they too don't want to be aligned with gay people. I've found blacks to be much more homophobic than whites, and many black churches have preachers who talk down any homosexual activity from the pulpit.

I didn't side with the rioters. I thought it was a shame and a tragedy because I saw firsthand what it was doing to my neighborhood. So many of our friends and family left Newark for the safer suburbs. Those who could afford it ran away without looking back, and the rest of us just held our breath and worried about the future. Nobody cared about our losses. They would say, "Well, you shouldn't be living there anyway, so move out." But we liked it there.

That was something most guys who hung downtown and who were from the suburbs didn't see. The riots destroyed all our Newark neighborhoods, and I mean all of them—black, white, Hispanic, mixed, and all the rest.

Businesses and professionals, including doctors, lawyers, and many local stores in the north and east areas that were considered safe, got their insurance revoked or raised through the roof. So they moved out of Newark, and we were left with very few businesses and professional services, not to mention so many good friends and relatives who also took the hint and left.

The whole downtown shopping area, once packed and thriving, became a ghost town. All the downtown activity and traffic were gone. Shoppers were afraid to go there for fear that the locals would take out their frustrations on them. And they were right. Many who did brave it got mugged. It was as if the locals thought they had the right to mug and terrorize shoppers.

No one went to the Waldorf anymore, and it soon closed. Almost every business closed except for the larger department stores, even though they lost most of their customers for good. Bamberger's eventually became Macy's, although changing the name didn't help much.

With or without the Newark riots, the malls became the place to go, although I'm sure that the fear of going into the city to shop helped bring it on.

And that was the end of Newark's heyday. Those of us who stayed were the lonely survivors of the riots and their aftermath, the outright destruction of our neighborhoods and way of life.

Chapter 20:
Tough Tony

It was 1970 now, and boy had Newark changed.

It was a sad time for me. My whole world had died with those riots, and I was so mad at those who caused them. It wasn't the fault of the local residents, because I remember all the out-of state-license plates on cars parked around the city that summer. The locals were caught in the middle and got hurt.

During the violence, the only protection many citizens of all races had in the north and east wards was from local Italian American groups, like the North Ward Citizens' Committee and its leader, Anthony "Tough Tony" Imperiale. I was a part of that movement. We had black people with us, and we had Hispanic people with us, although the majority were Italians.

The rap on Tony was that he was racist, but that was the furthest thing from the truth. Tony was a great guy and civic leader, and he did a lot for the poor residents of every race. His ambulance squad was a Godsend, and he didn't discriminate. He struck fear in the hearts of criminal types who otherwise would have done great harm to us. If a drug dealer or a gang member was terrorizing someone, we took care of it ourselves. We didn't need the cops. And that helped everyone, not just white people.

An ex-marine, Tough Tony was a stout and strong guy who had hands like a monster. He'd go up to someone he was arguing with, gently put his hand on the guy's shoulder, and squeeze so hard it would cause damage. But being full of pride, they usually wouldn't show they were hurt. They'd simply walk away, ending the argument.

No doubt, Tony had his enemies. One situation that puzzled me was the violent death of two of our closest supporters, Ray Gandi and Ralph Esposito. Ray was found on Bloomfield Avenue by Biasi's Restaurant. Someone had busted his head wide open with what could have been a baseball bat, and Ralphie was stabbed to death somewhere on Seventh Avenue in the old first ward. But it was taboo to look too closely into their deaths.

Tony knew I was bi, but he didn't give a damn. It meant nothing to him. He used to joke with me about it but wasn't prejudiced against me in the least. He just thought I wanted to stick my dick in everything, which was the truth.

Many different types of people joined the ranks of the North Ward Citizens' Committee (or NWCC), but as I said before, most of us were of Italian descent.

The nature of Italian Americans then was to be pro-family and pro-America, with God and family above all. Today, the Americans of Italian descent aren't a pimple on our asses. They watch TV programs like *The Sopranos* and fantasize about being tough mobsters and having their own crew. I remember some writer for *The Sopranos* eavesdropping on a conversation that Tony Imperiale was having with us at the Conca Doro Café. He was writing down our words to use in his script. So Tony finally said in Italian, "Be careful, he's writing everything down."

That mob stuff is enough to satisfy the pride of today's Italians in their nationality and history. They don't care about the real and lasting things Italians brought to this country. It's the same with rap music, that Neanderthal grunt and groan bullshit about death, murda, rape, and hate. It makes its listeners feel tough enough to satisfy their hunger for being cool and bad.

Back in Newark we were a true force to be dealt with, and we knew it.

Tony ran for and won an at-large (citywide) council seat in Newark and went on to make history in New Jersey by winning a state assembly seat in 1971 and then a state senate seat in 1973, both as an independent.

Of course, the local county Democratic Party, headed up by some senile old clerk named Nick Caputo, buried Tony's name on the bottom of the ballot. But we used that in our favor by shouting on our loudspeakers throughout the thirteenth legislative district, "Start at the bottom in the voting booth, just like how we struggled in life."

Boy did they howl and whine when we defeated them soundly that year. Tony got the top vote, and I found a new love for local and state politics.

I made lots of new friends in the close-knit organization that formed around the elections and our protests. So many people looked up to our movement and loved what we were doing, but others called us mobsters and vigilantes and thugs. We always wound up downtown, picketing city hall or some politician who was selling us out. I never made a dime working in those elections, and I was used for all I was worth. But I knew it and didn't mind, since it was something I loved and believed in. I was always doing it for the cause and lost a lot of precious time and youth because of that part of my personality.

Then came the Christmas when Tony won the election to the New Jersey state senate. Mom and I didn't have much of a holiday because I was busy electioneering through early November and didn't hold a job. It made me realize I was once again spinning my wheels and that I had to forge ahead and find new interests. I made a few attempts at running for office myself, but it never got me anywhere.

The money was short, so my election campaign didn't go as far as I wanted it to go. The funny thing is, I came very close to beating the entrenched Democrat Michael Adubato for a state assembly seat, whose brother was the powerful north Newark Democratic Chair. They didn't like that at all. I know Michael's influence has given me trouble with my current business, but that's okay too.

The whole game had become something else anyway, because once Tony Imperiale got elected there were these new people around him. One in particular took total control and squeezed the rest of us out. Funny, but now that I think about it, one guy who went to Tony's aid was sent by none other than Dick "The Prick" Spina, so I should have known.

The way the people around Tony in the state legislative office handled any problem was to "lay some shit on their heads," which meant to bullshit the people. They would bark a command to some minion in front of the person asking for help. They would end it with "mb," which meant "make believe."

The elections became more about what people could grab for themselves, rather than what we could do for our people. I wasn't interested in that at all, being a true believer then and still to this day.

There was this one guy who was with Tony from the start. His name was Moose Modica, and he was a real person. I liked Moosie, as we called him, and he liked me back. He and no one else knew all the other sides of me. Local politics was another of the separate lives I lived, but it was cool. Most of my life I felt like this secret agent, juggling work, home, politics, the navy, and the secret gay part.

Moose would always joke about the rotten cars I sold, but Moosie always bought cars from me

Right after the Newark riots, Ole Blue Ass (as I called Frank Sinatra) came to Newark because Symphony Hall had signed him to a contract before Newark had its problem. He had to honor it or

127

pay them a big fine. So, being the big tough Mafia-connected prick that Frankie Blue Ass was, he wanted protection for his lily-white Hollywood butt.

So who does he call? Tony Imperiale, of course!

His "guys" asked for a good bodyguard who knew Newark and could get Frankie around safely. There were no "wise guys" like that around, I guess.

Tony gave them Moosie, who was our biggest and most imposing guy and who packed a legal gun. Moosie traveled with Sinatra all weekend, and when the concerts were done, he took Frank to the airport. Mind you, this was all free for Ole Blue Ass, who never liked to pay for anything.

On boarding his plane, Old Blue turned to Moose and said in his creepy, know-it-all way, "You did a great job, kid. What kind of car do you drive?" So Moose said, "I'm a big guy, Frank. I drive a Lincoln."

"You got a brand new one," Frank barked back and then boarded his plane.

But guess what? Moose never got a new Lincoln, let alone a thank you note, from that cheap asshole. What do you expect from a guy like Ole Blue, who was invited to his hometown of Hoboken every year for their annual Sinatra celebration and never once showed up?

Don't get me wrong. I know I could never sway even one person to dislike Sinatra the legend. The legend did wonders for Italian Americans in this country, but Sinatra the man did nothing for anyone but himself. The character of Vito Corleone in *The Godfather*, which was a compilation of many mobsters and their lives, depicts Ole Blue Eyes better than the legend does.

The whole Tommy and Jimmy Dorsey thing that played out in that movie, where Johnny Fontaine couldn't get the film role, was Sinatra wanting to be in *From Here to Eternity* and not being able to get out of the contract he had signed with the Dorsey Brothers before he became so popular. Little Frankie Big shot sang the theme song for that movie.

His godfather wasn't Vito Corleone, but some local New Jersey don known as Richie the Boot, from his bootlegging days during Prohibition. Every Italian in Newark knew the story about the offer the Dorsey brothers couldn't refuse to release Sinatra from his contract, but that doesn't make Ole Blue a tough guy. It just made him the godson of a tough guy.

He was that whiney crooner *The Godfather* portrayed him to be and nothing more. He didn't do anything for Italian Americans intentionally. During my younger years there were rumors that his song "Strangers in the Night" referred to a gay man he dated very quietly back in the '60s. The song, the rumor said, was about how gay men cruise or show interest in each other by exchanging glances.

Funny, but I can't picture him with another man, although he was known in Hollywood for his legendary salami.

Like Moosie, Rose Visoskas, the mother of my friend Paul Rose, was heavily involved in our local community movement. Rose worked at Capri Italian Bakery, which boasted the best pignolli cookies. These neighborhood bakeries were as busy as beehives during the Easter and Christmas holidays.

There came a day when the Communist Party decided to support the local efforts of Amiri Baraka (LeRoi Jones) who was trying to build a low-income housing project called the Kawaida Towers. The plan was to put a socialist monument or high-rise where Baraka could operate his anti-American, anti-everything-we-believed-in type of organization. The only problem was they were building it in the middle of our Italian American neighborhood. So our organization went out to greet the commies supporting the tower.

Rose Senior, as we called Paul's mom, was among many older Italian woman who had umbrellas because of the rain that day, and somehow those umbrellas wound up on the heads of the commies. It was funny as hell.

At one point Rose asked one commie female if she was okay, since she had been hit on the head and was rubbing her bumps, but before the girl could answer, Rose asked, "Are you with them?" (Meaning the commies). The foolish girl nodded her head yes.

So Rose hit her on the head again, saying, "Good, now go back to Russia or Cuba, you little bitch!"

Chapter 21:
Kids Today

How sheltered and naive our young people are today. Even when they go to the ghettos to buy drugs and whores and get hurt, they excuse it away by saying, "Oh yeah, but there were these others who helped me get an ambulance."

They are all wannabes. I wannabe a millionaire before I'm thirty. I wannabe be a tough man and a rap star. Music and movies have become their religion, politics, and lifestyle. When did they change from being simple entertainment to becoming God?

None of the young people want to be themselves. Music and movies are their deities, and nothing much else matters to them. The pied piper of MTV has got them by the brain and won't let go.

They're not proud of their ancestry, their parents, their grandparents, or their heritage. That's why I want to start a heritage league for youth.

History means nothing them, although they can run a computer, tear it apart, and rebuild it. They don't know the basic realities that made this world what it is and how to keep it solvent and stable for their future and their children's future.

Generations X and Y and the latest one, Generation Whatever, have not a care in the world . . .

"Wanna go to a movie or do a black dude or drive to Atlantic City or have a three-way with two other guys or two girls or both?"

"Whatever."

They seem to get their satisfaction from shocking others rather than from something they succeeded at when nobody thought they could. They remind me of the Woodstock-type hippies of the '60s—plastering posters of their beloved Chairman Mao, who would slaughter them back in China if they put up pictures of Nixon or JFK.

My nephew was once crying to me about how he got a smack for his birthday some twenty years earlier from his father (Paulie) and how it affected his life. I told him he should forget the past and only look to the future. Then, without thinking about it, I blurted out what I believe to be one of my best lines.

"Forget the past, worry about the future. That's why God placed everything important on the front of your body, and only your ass in the back."

Unfortunately it didn't sink in, and he's still a lifelong problem.

Ah, that desire to make something from nothing is what drives me. Throughout my life, therein has been my success. It was a natural thing for me to be attracted to a failed business and turn it around. I did it a few times with much success and enjoyed watching it happen.

Want to know how I do it? My pleasure. Find a closed restaurant, bar, or store front, decide what you could do with it, and approach the landlord. Don't bother with the corporate guys because they have one set way of doing business and no wiggle room. Offer an earnest deposit for a lease and explain that you need time to organize your financing, but be sure you know what you're talking about. Say, "I have this plan for a great club or bar or shoe store, and I have the experience or the knowledgeable partners with money, and I just need a little time to get it together, but I don't want to lose this space you have for lease."

Do yourself a favor and do not rely on your friends. Do not take their advice. Every time I've tried to do something, all my friends tried to talk me out of it because most people don't have that entrepreneurial drive and feel more comfortable working for the man and having that paycheck every week. I didn't listen to anyone but my own head and heart, and I've had numerous successes because of that fact.

I had some failures, too, but it was an education, as my Jewish friends would say: "You paid for your education, and you don't do that again."

The Italian version is, "Uh oh, stay away from him, he went bad," like I was this rotten piece of fruit with brown spots all over it. I prefer and love the Jewish way of accepting failure: it makes sense.

But young people now don't want to learn how to succeed from their failures. It's as if they want to fail, be petted on the head and told it isn't their fault and everything will be fine.

What a bunch of jerk offs young people are, to drop everything and throw their lives to the dogs, doing drugs, having sex, and making babies with lowlifes as they follow their pied piper, MTV.

What is it with these young people today who want to be street thugs? They think you aren't cool unless you're a thug and preferably of a minority race. I was taught to be proud of my heritage, and I still am. My ancestors were at the pinnacle of class and culture, being of royal blood and involved in the arts, opera, and winemaking.

How sad it makes me to see more than two thousand years of European culture go down the drain. To me, music is simply entertainment and not a fantasy to make you cool, bad, or tough, or to control your thoughts, deeds, wants, and desires.

Lately I've met young people who claim to be born-again Christians, but it's only a scam to get you to drop your guard so they can sell you something worthless and make a year's pay, go home, and watch MTV. It's a new version of the old, "I know you're connected to the Mafia, so give me a loan" baloney. After I figured it out, I started calling them born-again Bullshitters right to their faces. Their only response was to laugh because they knew I was right.

Oh that Gen-X fool who kept telling everyone he was going to be a millionaire before his thirtieth birthday. He's thirty-three and still not a millionaire. This guy has introduced me to so many scammers—from an accountant who kept double billing me huge amounts to a contractor who took a deposit and disappeared because I believed their born-again baloney.

How people can take the good name of a Christian movement and use it for their own scamming games is unbelievable to me. I found out later that this clown was getting a piece of everything he sent me. That would be fine if he sent good people who charged a fair price and did the job I hired them to do. But it was all about how much money they could extract from me. He'd hang around me to scam information he could use to glean even more money from me.

Thank God I have a good mind and don't have to resort to seedy tricks to grab money from friends and relatives.

Today people say and do anything they want without any conscience and never keep their word. I was taught that if you didn't keep your word, it would be a bad molokai, or a curse upon your future as well as all the generations to come.

Young people as a whole don't want to hear the wisdom of age and experience, having gone to Womb University. They really believe they were born with knowledge injected into their brains, like a memory stick or even a fully downloaded hard drive. Yes, they all know and have computers, but we were the generation that invented and built those same computers.

The youth of today believe in fantasy, like extraterrestrials and the Da Vinci code, but we who have been around for some decades know there are no little green men from outer space, nor are there any secrets or codes in the Holy Bible.

One of the saddest moments in my life was when John Lennon was killed.

Don't get me wrong. I never had any use for him or his song "Imagine," which went on to explain how much better the world would be without possessions and religion and every other thing I believed in.

It was just that shortly before Lennon's death, a wonderful, newly elected pope with a beautiful and honest smile died, and there were more candle lit rallies and processions for Lennon by far. That was when I knew this world was in trouble.

When Lennon died, his wife Yoko Ono said her husband was with God, but remembering "Imagine," with all of its anti-God, anti-individual rights statements, I said to myself, "Oh no he isn't. He's probably with the God of hell fire or the God of weed and bongs."

I blame a lot of programs, songs, and attitudes that were shoved down young people's throats and that forced independent thinkers to keep their opinions to themselves, not dare utter a controversial thought, nor show any love of God or pride in their country and ancestry. All this hypnotic pied piper trickery is now the duty of MTV and Hollywood. I think I was sleeping when they passed around the Kool-Aid because when I try to talk to people about the state of things, they look at me as if I'm from another planet or better yet, another universe. I now know that it's more like I'm from another time, when reality was the norm, when fantasy was kept for the children and fiction classics, and when some silly queen didn't transform into a cowboy by putting on western hat.

Young people today seem to be of one mind and believe in a McDonald's style of life where everything is prepackaged for you and you're told what's best for you. If anyone objects, they are "crazy" or "old school" or worse and should be avoided. Individualism is now considered stupid. Phony and plastic lives are the norm, and everyone is happy for it.

The best of our young people go to war, risking their futures and their lives for our country, while the rest of them watch MTV and become street thugs. Cool, huh? Or is it "kewl"?

When I was young, we had passion and beliefs and honor. We were decent and honest and had respect for all people of all races (and animals, too), and we didn't need any legislation or politically correct rules to do it.

Chapter 22:
More Downtown Memories

I want to go back to the days of downtown Newark, when you could go to any number of movie theatres, like the Capitol and the Paramount and the Lowes and the Branford and of course, the Proctor. It was an era we will never see again, and the movies were only part of the fun. You could meet a new flame or a quick sex partner or a funny new friend to hang out with.

It gives me more reason to miss my old dear downtown and my old dear world. The fun we had was something I don't see young people enjoying today.

Some of the people around then were really inspirational and didn't mind sharing their knowledge with an interested young person. True, there were some who were hoping it would help them to get into your young pants, but you could still learn from them.

I remember Chickie barking at some old gentleman after the guy asked what book he was reading. He was interested in what young people liked to read. It upset me that Chickie couldn't give the old man a civil answer.

But then there were the funny scenes and characters, like the Cleanup Woman, who was really a gay guy but had these awful bangs and wiry way about him.

I called him that because he'd go down on four or five guys a night, right there on track three. Sometimes the railroad police arrested him, but that never stopped him. The excitement of possibly getting caught drew him on like a moth to a flame.

He told me he thought the bangs made him look like a little Dutch boy, but they really made him look like an old maid auntie who cleaned other people's houses for a living. I gave him the name Cleanup Woman not for his looks but for his actions on track three.

Funny, but years later there was a song of the same name about a woman who would scoop up your man if you didn't want him, and those of us who remembered him laughed whenever we heard it.

Then there was Dement, so named because he was simply demented and odd. He'd tell us stories of getting caught by people in office buildings when he was on his knees to some young man. He'd give us the details as coolly and calmly as if he were relating a funny movie he'd seen.

The story that sticks in my head is the one about him in an elevator with a sailor in the National Newark and Essex Bank on Broad Street, with Dement on his knees doing his usual thing. As the elevator went up, Dement went down, not thinking that it would stop on floors other than the one he pushed. Of course it did, and there was a crowd of businesspeople ready to board staring at him and his sailor.

So Dement, without taking the guy's dick out of his mouth, turned to look at the horrified crowd. Then a delayed reaction kicked in, and Dement pushed the sailor away, and ran out of the elevator. Demented for sure.

It struck me as funny that most guys I knew would hate it if a straight guy they met wanted to go down on them, but I liked it that way.

Transistor Sister was another funny one. He would stroll around downtown with this huge radio strapped to his back, constantly playing the latest rock and roll hits. You knew he was coming for miles because you heard him long before you saw him.

I caught the whole act one day as he was getting baffed on track 3 by a big blond, who turned out to be an Aussie traveling through to a Future Farmers of America meeting, of all things. They were screwing to the tune of the music, and I got some real comic relief.

The Aussie had a tool on him like I never saw on or off the screen. It had to be over twelve inches and as fat as an Italian Genoa salami. I figured that no woman could handle it, so he hunted out guys who would jump at the chance of conquering that monstrosity. The Aussie kept drilling Transistor Sister to the tune of "When Johnny Comes Marching Home" or some other war song from either the First or Second World War. How Transistor Sister took that thing I don't know, but he sure did scream a lot.

I never could see what the fuck the guy on the receiving end got out of it, but it was explained to me that "it hurt so good."

Howdy Doody was another one, with his red hair, freckles, crackling voice, and oh that blotchy complexion. He would prance around Penn Station with his arms folded as he walked, which made him look so obviously gay, and chase after men going into the men's room.

Howdy begged me to introduce him to this gang of four Italian American and Polish boys from the Ironbound that I hung around with, because he wanted to suck them all off. An hour or so later I ran into him stumbling down Raymond Boulevard, bloody and bruised in the rain.

I asked what happened, and he said they took him to an isolated construction area with the promise of dick and then beat him with a hubcap they found there. Feeling responsible, I gave him cab fare to get home, but I must admit he looked like Anna Magnani from her movie *The Rose Tattoo*. I told him that a few days later, along with the Penny's (Penn Station) crowd. We all got a good laugh from it.

One fine night the Newark version of the Gestapo arrested Howdy Doody in Washington Park. We heard him screaming, *"I'm not a cock sucker! I'm not a cock sucker!"* over and over again as they dragged him away.

Nothing could have been further from the truth.

Once my friend Don was in the laundry room of his high-rise in Newark, and a real classy lady was having a cultured conversation with him about opera and the arts. Then Don pulled a rolled-up bath towel from his laundry bag, and out popped this enormous double-headed dildo that flopped, one head at a time, toward the woman.

Don tried to cover it up: "Oh no! Where could that have come from?" I joked that she probably knew exactly where it came from.

And then there was the time Don needed his phones rewired and told the building's super to let in the phone guys while he was at work. When Don got home that night, he saw that his bed had been moved so the phone man could get to the jacks. Dildos of all shapes, sizes, and colors were lying around. The phone guys left them that way to let Don know they saw them.

In his older days, Don, like many older gay men, took on the persona of a ninety-year-old female, or what I call the "granny goose syndrome." For example, when working at the door of my nudie bar, he'd throw his hands up whenever there was a problem and shout, "Oh no, what are we gonna *dooooooooooo?*

It could be the most minor situation, like giving a customer too little change or the dancer not getting the pizza she ordered, but whatever the problem, Don put on his act.

Howdy Doody, the Great Frog, and most guys from the suburbs were very well educated and well read, so they would stand in front of Penn Station and argue current events and politics for hours. But they were really there for one reason only: men and moremen. Whenever a man looking for sex showed up, all the talking stopped, and they turned into big cats in the jungle vying for the next prey.

It was okay, I guess, because in reality it was life and what made the world go round, for gay people anyway.

There are so many sub stories I remember that it's hard to describe some of them, like the Halloween that I, the big manly man, decided at the last minute to go in drag and shock all my downtown friends.

I got this old poison green dress my sister gave me, since by then she was a buxom blonde, and an old wig wag or wig hat that was popular then, and had her make me up.

So downtown I went to Skippy's Hideaway, an old bar and grill turned gay out of desperation, which was the norm for most gay bars, and shock I did.

They were screaming, "What? Bob the sailor? Is that really you?"

Everyone—and I mean all of them—said I looked like Shelly Winters, who wasn't so bad looking in those days as the most famous of all the buxom blondes. With my poison green dress and black cotton wig wag, I was dancing to Otis Redding's version of "Satisfaction," its high screaming notes of shock befitting a butch guy gone drag

Arching my back and bumping and grinding my friends, they howled at the sight of me as a woman. What a fun night it was. I even stopped at the Howard Johnson's rest area in Union on the Garden State Parkway, which is still a cruise area, and shocked everyone there.

Funny, but it wasn't talked about after that night. I guess I busted a bubble for everyone who hoped the gay community would "act more manly."

On the way home to take off that dress and makeup, an old john who I'd seen in the past approached me. Wow, this dude was weird. He wanted me to screw him wearing the dress while I called myself Marilyn. So I got him to pay extra, and Marilyn screwed him while talking as dirty as she could.

I would always rather turn a buck than have a fun time with sex, and fifty dollars was a lot of money in 1964—especially for me.

Chapter 23:
Darren and Stash

So many times I've tried to find a place where 1963 was still alive and a downtown like Newark's was still thriving, but all I hear from people is that I should move to Australia or some other faraway land.

I wanted and tried to recreate that atmosphere in my own businesses and did have some success, especially at the Cactus Club in Newark, where there was a friendly and wholesome attitude among the staff and regular customers. I always paid serious money to off-duty Newark policemen and women to keep my customers safe (unlike other gay clubs). But that atmosphere was fleeting, and I found that after the club closed, the friendships we had forged melted away into memory. Those whose companionship I treasured stopped calling. Some even snubbed me when I ran into them, as if I had done something wrong.

The worst of it was the wake of my dear love and friend Darren, who worked as a bartender at all my clubs and was truly the love of my life.

I met him at Feathers, where I saw him staring into his drink in a way that revealed his loneliness and depression. So I asked him to dance, and we became lovers. We saw each other every night for a few years, making love at every chance.

But it seemed as if the so-called gay community thought I had done something wrong, as they snubbed me at Darren's wake and funeral. Funny thing is, all the straight people there were consoling me, but all the gays I had been friendly with acted like I was the reason Darren died from AIDS, which was the furthest thing from the truth.

I tried and tried to stop him from going to those all-night parties in Manhattan. I watched him waste away into a splotchy, gray-skinned, blind skeleton, and if anyone didn't deserve that it was Darren, because he was the sweetest guy.

He was so easily used by his idiot bar friends, and it hurt to see him being led like a lamb to the slaughterhouse. Those so-called friends dragged him into Manhattan with limos and drugs, where Darren got involved in unsafe sex, so I guess they didn't want to hear from me at his wake.

He was so lovable that I used to call him my "little bear." But his gay bar friends talked him out of our affair, saying it was childish and silly and that he could do so much better in New York. Yeah, right! He did so well he died of AIDS. I guess that's why they all avoided me after he died.

That's part of the problem I have with gay men. Too many of them like to break up couples and see everyone miserable and heartbroken.

Though Darren was the love of my life, Stash was my first love and the other ex I had to watch die a horrible death from AIDS. If Darren was the sweetest guy, Stash was the most promiscuous man I ever knew, and he made no bones about it.

It was a sorry day when he called me from Cabrini Hospital in Manhattan and started crying, "I don't want to die." I found out the next morning that I was the last person to talk to him, and that's how he wanted it.

Stash and I met in a gay bar in Asbury Park called The Oddisy, after my friend Anthony pushed me into him so we would have to talk to each other. We danced and kissed and wound up in my car with our pants down, and from then on we were lovers. Stash was very much into designer clothes, and we started wearing Calvin Klein jeans long before they were popular. When I went around my Nicky Newark Guido crowd, they'd ask me why I was wearing a Jew's name on the back of my jeans. I was quick to reply that they would be wearing them next year, and sure enough they were.

Stash and I broke up because all my friends kept telling him that if he went to New York he'd become a star. After we started going out, Stash spent most nights sleeping over in "the city" because he might have modeling interviews the next morning. Oh, but that didn't mean he was sleeping around (oh no, not at all). Eventually I got mad enough and broke up with him. It also broke my heart.

After Stash worked a few years at Mays Department Store, I teased him by singing my version of the store's jingle: "At Mays each day, a sale day, all day long . . . and twenty million lowlifes can't be wrong." Poor Stash never made any real money and never became a star on Broadway (maybe in Paterson or Passaic). It hurt to see him struggle. He was a good person, but as with most gays, the call of the Big Apple robbed him of his health and eventually his life.

After he died, his mother scattered his ashes around my lake. She thought it was the best place for them to be. I agreed, since that's where I scattered my Luigi Bear's ashes, and Stash loved that dog. It's funny how Darren, Stash, and I were all big dog lovers.

My poor, sweet Darren. He never had real sex with another man before me. He was so good and so beautiful to me. I miss my little bear. He was the little bear who made me care. They don't make young men like my little Darren bear anymore.

I tried to preach to both Darren and Stash that there were diseases out in the gay community that science and doctors hadn't even heard of yet, but they scoffed at me. Years later, when Stash had

AIDS, I reminded him of that statement. He tried to put me down in front of a phony hairdresser friend named Ray Ray. Stash laughed, because Ray Ray wiped his lips as if he had just finished having oral sex. But I pressed the issue, telling Stash that in his case I had been right. He just hung his head in sorrow, which made me sorry I had reminded him.

Ray (or "Ray Ray," so nice they named her twice) was a typical fag who told both Stash and Darren that they should go to New York and that I was "holding them back." Words of wisdom from a typical old queen with her microwaveable dinners and five cats, all alone with straight divorcee females, whose hair he did to make ends meet.

What an idiot.

Chapter 24:
More Sexcapades

Years ago, New York had parking areas and docks where trucks would park and where you'd have crowds of men having sex with each other. You could go there any night and see a show that no porn video could match in excitement. But of course, the NYPD had to come and destroy our fun because it was long before Stonewall and we were an easy target.

One night I watched as the police raided the docks. I wasn't in the action area, so I felt thrilled that I wasn't the one getting arrested and was actually gloating over some friends who were. So what goes around comes around. A few weeks later I was arrested, and since I was in the navy, I threw my ID out the police station window. Since I was the manly one hanging out with some older, feminine queen, they charged us under the now-defunct sodomy law, claiming he was blowing me while everyone else watched. The truth was, nobody was doing anything but standing around. Yet these two police rookies decided to ruin our lives with their lies. To this day, whenever my record is checked, I have to explain it. I hope those two bastards have really fem gay sons and eventually burn in hell.

I'm convinced that they, like most men who harass gays, were and are latent homosexuals who need to prove they aren't to the world around them. Otherwise, why would they lie about what we were doing when we weren't doing anything at all? One of the two arresting officers followed me into the men's room at the precinct and blatantly checked out my three-piece set. I confronted him at one point, asking why he lied and wanted to ruin our lives. He just gave me a blank stare.

The areas I frequented the most and where I met the most sex partners were the two Howard Johnsons on the Garden State Parkway. One was in Union of all places, and the other was in Bloomfield. They're now run by McDonald's, which is much less tolerant than Ho Jo's was.

I'd meet married and straight men on their way home from their jobs, or a bar, or a hot date that didn't get them any sex. Women in the '60s and even '70s were much less promiscuous than they are today, or at least for the first few dates, which left men horny as hell. So they'd go to Ho Jo's for oral sex and a quickie, usually with a fem dude.

That's where Big Bobby came in. I was in great demand because guys wanted it from another butch guy and not a girlie type. I'm not saying there aren't exceptions to that rule, but given a choice between some girlie queen and me, most guys would choose me. This made me even less popular among the regular crowd than I usually was.

There was this cute young bus boy at the Ho Jo's who I liked, and I mentioned him to the waitress I was friendly with. She said I shouldn't try anything with him because his family was involved with the local church that was trying to get the politicians to clean up Ho Jo's and stop those evil, satanic fags from hanging out. Well, as luck would have it, this young man was sitting on the ledge outside the place one night waiting for a ride home. I was just hanging out there without even a thought that he might be interested in me when he asked if I could give him a ride home.

I asked where he lived and he said the next town over, so I told him I would. He wasn't in my car for a minute when he said I should take out that big one of mine. When I asked him how he knew I had a big one, he explained that he had looked through the exhaust fan in the men's room, like the state police did to catch men having sex. So I took it out, and the rest is history.

I was a little shaken, too, because I wondered if the troopers had caught me jerking it that night at the urinals, showing off to some queen who wanted it, but it worked out better because I got to have little Barry Big Cock on his knees. His huge salami, which Mom and Dad graced him with to use on females, was laid to waste while he serviced my dick. Whoa, what a turn on that was.

He sucked me dry and then pulled his pants down to jerk off. Whoa, this skinny, frail, pale boy had enough meat to feed the poor. He said his family came here on the Mayflower, and I joked that they brought that salami with them.

He had left his white Ho Jo uniform in my car, so I brought it back to Ho Jo's and gave it to the waitress (who we had nicknamed Mrs. Butterworth, after the pancake syrup). I told her I found it outside, and she said, "Oh, this must belong to little Barry, because it's small and he's the smallest man here."

So I barked back, "Little? That's what you think, but you're dead wrong, lady," knowing it would shock and amuse her. I told her all the gory details, and we laughed about it for years, especially about what his homophobic family would think if they knew that dear little Barry was doing a dirty dude who hung out at that horrible place.

For years, Barry and I had wild sex and three ways with other men and yes, even some straight couples. It was hot because I was the big man type and he was the little boy type. Many a night we'd go to Ho Jo's and pick up a drunken so-called straight guy in the men's room, drag him back to my house down the street, and have our way with him. Then we would go out for coffee and laugh about it for hours into the night. Barry and I always made sure we got him to be on the bottom for both of us, one at a time or together. We even had a few who would look for us and try to get with us again. Guys used to go nuts for our big things—it was like the biggest taboo for them. Boy, did I ever feel alive after one of those sessions. Then they'd go home to some female and make love to her.

One time some dude's girlfriend or wife followed him to my house and banged on my door. When I answered, she started screaming that I made her husband gay. I told her I had given him little pink pills and remarked on what a nice body he had. She tried to scratch my face.

With that, her husband came out and put her in his car, and little Barry followed them home in the wife's car. After a few hours Barry returned with the guy and we finished up. What a story they told of her crying and screaming that her (Irish) family was Mafia and that she was going to get me killed. The sex with her husband was that much hotter as I thought of her screaming about me back home.

Chapter 25:
Sex vs. Love

During my life I've met many types of men and women from different walks of life, from police to military people, from professors of political science to lawyers and doctors and other professionals. And from that experience, I must conclude that all men, regardless of their education or social standing, are dogs. Most will screw an orange if they think no one is watching. Of course, the rest of us will scorn the man caught screwing the orange but then go home and masturbate thinking about it.

Or maybe masturbate about doing the orange *with* the guy, or maybe just doing a girl with the orange, or maybe the guy *with* the girl and the orange, or perhaps just the guy.

As I said before, men are dogs and will do anything to excite themselves, their female partner, or their male partner. So there it is.

Women are no better, except they hide it well. But men get a throb in their pants just by revealing their inner thoughts and desires. It's weird how they get excited over the slightest little thing but then act like I'm the nutty one. But I usually let it slide for peace's sake.

I wonder if most people have ever experienced the joy of love and sex with someone they have true feelings for. I hate how they excuse away anonymous sex with the filthiest street scum by saying, "It's only sex." You then go home and kiss your wife, girlfriend, or mother with that same mouth?

Don't get me wrong. I'm no angel. I've had anonymous sex with many men and women I didn't know or care to know. But to be monogamous with someone special was a warm feeling I never felt with anonymous sex.

I mean, I could always get relief from the clean up Woman or Mister Machine, who was so good at it that guys would line up for him. Or I could always find a glory hole at some filthy adult bookstore, where high school seniors and college guys came to suck off married or retired guys, and then sit on your penis as it stuck through the hole while watching straight and gay porn.

But none of this was nearly as thrilling as doing it with someone you knew and cared for.

I may have been promiscuous, but I also drew the line at certain kinds of behavior. I've always made the attempt to avoid married men, married women, men of the cloth, and people who were close to marriage. If I did something like that, I felt very funny about it, very dirty and guilty. I don't know where that came from, perhaps from my parents, but I felt very bad about that kind of behavior. And I didn't want to be in the middle of that for five minutes of fun.

Most people will do anything with anybody at any time and not give a shit who they hurt. And that's wrong.

Promiscuity and all the vices that come along with it are much more prevalent in the gay community because, unfortunately, there's not a lot to keep you tied down, like children, family, and the expectations of society. Gay men, in particular, are a little bit too free. I've seen gays who wouldn't even consider being with a woman go after married men. They don't care if he has a lovely wife and is raising a nice family. It's all about their five minutes of fame. Gays are hated enough already. Why give the heterosexual community even more fodder to hate you? If you want the world to respect you, respect yourself and respect each other. And if you can't do that, you're never going to get respect from this world. That's why I never liked or went to these totally gay-controlled haunts.

The biggest problem I have with the gay community is that they get bored with everything very, very quickly. They're like weather vanes—the slightest wind turns their attention in another direction. The word that has stood the test of time in the gay community is "next." Your lover of seven months is leaving you? Well, next! I lost my job, so next! There was even a gay magazine called *Next*, with that nasty she-she mentality that has always pissed me off. What a way to go through life. I hate all that next shit, man. I wanted and still want to be with someone for a long-term relationship but *nooooo*. Next! Next! And oh yes! Whatever!

Not all but many gays I have encountered throughout my life have the worst traits of both men and women. It's pitiful to see them live in misery just to prove they can be as bitchy as the next man or woman.

Friends are no help when they coax young guys to go to "the city," telling them they'll fit in there, have loads of hot men, get discovered, and become a model. Next! *Whatever!*

I've always been angry at the way some gay men (more former friends than strangers) would try, with their every bone and drop of blood, to hurt each other and separate happy couples. It was always done in a sneaky, underhanded way, disguised as something good for you.

For example, one so-called friend I won't name accompanied my partner and me to Florida, and being single himself, started telling us, "Oh, you two should go out there and meet other people, to see how much you really need each other" or "That guy over there has a lot of money and a big fat dick and likes you a lot." It was all made up just to separate us so he could sleep with my partner.

I know it happens in every walk of life, but it seems to me, observing both sides here, that gay men make it their passion and extract great joy by ruining good relationships between people who usually are their closest friends. It happens more in the gay community because gay men are vicious and jealous for the most part.

We had our troubles downtown at times, but it was always minor and didn't last long, like when bashers would try to terrorize us and get a few punches in. Or when the police decided they were bored and would harass and arrest us for no good reason.

I go online—which, by the way, along with the false acceptance of gays and the onslaught of pseudo-bisexuality, has ruined the gay bar industry—and meet guys who have the same likes as me. We talk for a few days and then poof! They're gone.

By pseudo-bisexuality, I mean that a lot of gays today think it's cool to say they like girls too when they're really totally gay. Even if they're not bisexual they'll tell you they are because it's "cool." I don't see a lot of straight guys saying they're bisexual.

The gay community is a land of make believe. It's all fantasy. It's all a joke. It's all "look at the cowboy!" My response? "That's not a cowboy—that's a fag in a cowboy hat." I've actually said that, but they prefer the fantasy to reality. But you know what? If you're twenty-one or older, grow up.

And this fantasy issue is more prevalent among the fems, because in their heart of hearts they would rather be a woman. Their theme song is "Someday My Prince Will Come." It's not so rampant among the butch gays, although they'll play the game to get along with everyone.

Gays can be so cruel to each other, and I don't know why. How can we expect the rest of humanity to respect and accept us if we don't respect each other? Blacks show respect for one another by using "brother" and "sister." Maybe we can use our own terms for each other, like "my man" or "guy" or "boy" or "bud." But not "Mary" or "Grace" or "girl," as the fems do.

Why can't gay men be like lesbians? Many gay female couples last for many, many years, like Judy and Phyllis and many other lesbian couples I knew. If we had more stable relationships, it would help our cause of being accepted by society and religion.

I can't explain why it doesn't work, but none of my relationships lasted, and it wasn't because of me. My partner always wanted to move on because he was bored with our relationship and wanted more than I could offer him. And as I've said, his friends were always telling him he could do better and that I was holding him back from being someone famous or whatever. What in the hell is wrong with young gay people that they even believe this crap?

Maybe that's why I kept taking my gay again straight again boyfriend Hank back. I knew there was no hope for a real relationship in my life with another man or woman, so I hung on to the play-act phony one I had.

My friend Don's ghost got Hank back for me on a recent Thanksgiving in front of my family when a knife jumped off the counter and cut his finger. (I guess Don knew Hank's plans to dump me.) As Hank was talking to me about it the next morning, coffee splashed out of his cup and all over his face, as if an invisible hand did it. Thanks again, Don!

The people I love sometimes do nasty things to me, and I think it's karma or payback for my conservative, less flamboyant way of life, and because of who I do and do not accept into my life. At the same time, nasty things also happen to the people I love. Maybe it's wishful thinking, but I doubt these recurring situations are happening in true reality. I believe they're happening in some kind of alternate reality.

In the true realm of reality, my friends are living good, healthy, and normal lives. Stash is a big star, Darren is a baseball player, Hank is a lawyer with three children and a wonderful wife who loves him, and all these horrible things I keep trying to save them from aren't real to anyone but me. Maybe this is to teach me to be more tolerant of people and their misgivings, but I am what I am, as the song goes.

I actually had a spiritual experience once when I visited Darren's grave on his birthday. It was pouring rain, and I was so broke and out of options that I got down on my knees, pressed my face against his tombstone, and began to cry. I was asking for his help. Right then I felt this jolt from the stone through my body.

Not soon after, I got the club Hott 22 (which was the second coming of the Cactus Club) from a nice old guy named Danny Williams on the promise I would make it work. I guess I have to thank Darren for that one.

Chapter 26:
Homophobia and Stereotypes

One fine day when I was just out of high school, I got a firsthand taste of homophobia. I was living on Garside Street, and my mom and I were just entering the second-floor apartment we had rented. This was just after I had left school to go to work so we could eat and pay the bills.

It seems that Johnny Derange, that cute little German American boy from high school who outed me after I had sex with him, forcing me to leave Barringer High, wanted to get one last lick in. He wanted to prove to all his friends, without a doubt, that he wasn't interested in anything I had to offer him sexually. So they decided to parade down the middle of Garside Street, screaming "fag" at me over and over in high-pitched voices, right in front of Mom. She was confused and fortunately didn't hear their words, so I told her to go inside and I shut the door behind us.

I waited months and months for them to return so I could use the baseball bat I had placed just inside our front door, but they never came back. I guess Johnny proved his point to his jerk-off friends. Homophobia wasn't even a known word in the early '60s. Everyone thought it was okay and cool to harass a "faggot" and show him who's boss and who's the man. How ignorant they were. I only wish his friends were there when Johnny was romping on my big manhood and moaning in ecstasy.

I've always hated how we've been harassed and stereotyped. That high-pitched voice shit is one of the worst stereotypes and has haunted me for much of my life. The extremely fem guys were the ones everyone noticed, so straight, fag-hating, and closet gay America put me in the same pot as the fems. And then the homophobes had the upper hand and made me their trophy.

Some of my closest straight friends, who made up 90 percent of all my friends, had that same nasty fem-imitating habit until I corrected them and asked them if they ever heard me act or talk like that. If they didn't hear my anger and kept up the annoying girly mimicking act, I'd cut them off until I either got an apology or until they got the message and stopped calling or contacting me. Then the rest of my friends would hear about it and be on guard not to fucking try and use that Fairy Mary shit on me.

The funny thing is that I inherited my dad's anger. He'd throw the closest thing he could reach at you, and my friends all knew I'd do the same thing. So they would watch their words, and if that turned them off to the point of not talking to me anymore, that was okay, too.

One night I saw some stupid girl and her friends squeezing their way through the crowd at Feathers (that gay bar in River Edge, New Jersey). She said in a high-pitched voice to all the guys, "Oh, excuse me, miss," so I made sure I was in her path of destruction. As she passed me, sure enough she said in that high-pitched voice, "Oh, excuse me, miss."

So I barked out in my deepest, loudest man voice, "Who the fuck are you calling miss, dyke?"

With that she apologized, and some gay guy said, "Hi, Dan the man," with a big smile of admiration. I always loved those Kodak moments. By then I was no longer Bobby but used my first name Dan, because I liked it better. It didn't sound little boy like Bob or Bobby.

Another big problem I've had through the years is why so many people laugh at the very mention of the word gay or when they see a group of obviously gay men. I know it isn't anywhere near as bad as it used to be, but it still exists in quiet little circles where I usually wind up. That's because I'm still assumed to be straight in some circles; well, at least before this book.

What the fuck is so god-damned funny? I've confronted people with that question when I've caught them laughing at me when I'm with gay friends, and they're not ready with an answer. I guess it's all part of the, "See, I'm laughing at the fags, so I can't be one" mentality.

Today gays are more accepted, but in my view it's largely a false acceptance. Gays are accepted because for many people "it's the thing to do" and they would be outcasts if they didn't accept them. And that's because being gay is very popular now. But the acceptance is not sincere. I can tell that by the way people act and talk around me. I can tell that they really don't like gays and are uncomfortable around them. They don't invite you to parties. When they see you on the street, they're very quick and abrupt. They'll date and marry blacks, but they can't be that way with guys of my ilk and beyond.

I was invited to wedding by a couple who claimed to be very open and accepting, and they sat me at the gay table with a bunch of queens. I didn't want to be segregated at the "gay table." I wanted to be treated like everyone else and celebrate their wedding, not be segregated like that. I didn't like it, and I let them know it.

Even the gay community never accepted me because I wasn't "gay enough." Some people have said that I'm really not gay, that I just like putting my dick in everyone. And you know what? I don't bother to identify myself. I don't think it's necessary anymore. There used to be a time when it was, but not anymore. The world has changed, and I really would prefer the old world, when we had our secret words and secret deeds and secret club. No one knew, and I liked it that way. Because it was real and it was honest. And I love honesty.

Many people I employed over the years, both gay and straight, took my sexuality as a reason to misjudge my strength and test me on a daily basis. I had to constantly prove to them that what I did in bed for ten minutes a few times a week didn't make me a pushover. My favorites were the young ones I had to confront when business was off. Unless they worked harder to sell and help me succeed, I told them, I would have to let them go. Their response was to find the nearest chair, put their feet up, and wait to be fired.

People have disrespected me in many ways. Once a big, fat dude named Pat, who I knew from the old neighborhood in Newark, started hanging around my club. For old times' sake, I let him come in for free. Pat decided to tell all of my dancers that he was the real owner and I just worked for him. This was fun for me, because I liked playing with people like him. One fine day my manager cornered me in the office and asked me if I was the true owner. He went on to explain that he got into an argument with a dancer and threatened her, saying that I wasn't happy with her leaving early and coming in late.

So she said, "Oh yeah? Well, Dan is not the real owner, anyway."

As my manager stared at her with a puzzled look on his face, she added, "Oh, you don't know, do you? Dan isn't the real owner. Pat owns this club, and Dan just works for him."

Now, this was a real problem for my day-to-day operation, because my manager and my security were wondering if it's true, and they started saluting this Fat Pat when he came in, which was three times a day now. So I told my nervous manager to go and tell this all-knowing dancer that she was dismissed and we would no longer honor her contract. If she didn't like it, she could go and tell Pat and he'd simply order me to reinstate her contract. Then I banned Pat the Fat from my club, and everyone sighed in relief.

Other employees stole as much as they could from me to build a nest egg on my ass. Those were the worst of all because they had no loyalty at all and didn't care if I failed. But even worse than that were the ones who acted sane and normal. Yes, they were just acting.

The only thing I've seen put cold water on the anti-gay fire is money. If you have a little money, you can do just about anything in this world (within reason) and be accepted. And if you don't have money, forget it.

Somehow I wish we could all be judged by our intelligence and not be dumped into one big stinky melting pot but *oh noooo!* It seems I'm always put in the same pot as the liberal gay hierarchy, which to the person votes, lives, and reacts in a liberal, far-left way. Many gay or bi people fall into this gay rut where they live out their lives the way the gay hierarchy and the ever-present liberal media want and expect them to.

But I never cared about that, preferring to be who I am and not interested in acceptance from anyone. Therein lies my rebel roots. Does anyone hear me when I say I want to be known as a good American and a good person, God-loving, and respectful of the law?

Most people assume that a gay person has to be an extreme liberal. I've voted for a Democrat when he or she was the best candidate, but for the most part I've always preferred independent candidates because I feel their views are better for this country. I've never voted for a candidate because they could help me personally but if only they were the best candidate for my country and its people.

You can ask 90 percent of the gay "community," and they will proudly shout back to you that they are extreme left-wing radicals. They think that will get them the precious rights they so crave. But I feel they go along with extreme politics just for the shock value, and they end up stereotyping themselves. To them every day is Halloween and role playing. Who they really are doesn't matter, because for them it's all about the fantasy and not the reality of life. Oh yes, the entire world revolves around them and always has. Don't come as you are but as you would be, and don't worry about what others think of you. Be outrageous to the limit and beyond, and the world will conform to your wishes.

What a crock. The world isn't your stage, and it certainly isn't one big Halloween drag show filled with gold lamé and tulle fabric and pretty bows and ribbons.

Gays seem to think that acceptance and change will happen if they rub their lives in everyone else's faces. I know it won't, because I have a better handle on the straight mentality than many totally gay, completely out men who seem to be out of touch with reality.

I never realized how bitter I could get about certain aspects of the gay community until I started writing this book. The community expects me to accept everyone and everything just because I'm bisexual, and I can't, because some of it is just a little too far-fetched for me.

I'm for gay rights, but I don't like the way it's being done. I can't stand the question, "If you're not a liberal Democrat, how can you be gay?" And I can be, because I know the Republicans are better for business, by far. The Democrats want to raise taxes on everyone who makes more than a million dollars. That's insane. The top 2 percent of the country already pays 60 percent of the taxes. And they want to tax them more? They're taxing the job makers.

The Democrats were always the party of the moochers who don't want to work. They're not the party of the people and of the poor. The Republicans are the party of the successful, and the Democrats are the party of the failures. They want unemployment, they want disability benefits, and they want checks in the mail without working. I grew up in a more self-sufficient time, and I prefer that.

Chapter 27:
Gay Rights

When gay marriage was briefly legalized in California in 2008, I saw a lesbian couple on TV rocking back and forth in joy. It was beautiful to watch, but I got a little upset because it's too late for me to enjoy that freedom. I wanted so badly to marry the person I loved, even with all of his faults. As the Billy Holiday song goes, "Taint nobody's business if I do." I won't get into all of the lyrics here, but that song fits my feelings.

But I'm happy that others can enjoy it now. When it comes to marrying someone we love, I don't think straight people should choose for me. After all, I didn't get to choose for them. As a devout individualist who embraced a bisexual life long before it was accepted or even en vogue, I always craved the respect and honor that so-called "normal" men and women commanded.

I was surprised when my Neanderthal niece put her two cents in and said she thought civil unions were better for gays. I told her civil unions would be better for straight people, too.

This family member also told me recently, while wrinkling her nose, that she "just didn't understand or get" gay people. Nor did she understand gay or bi sex, preferring "plain vanilla."

Well, how about this? Ya see how you're attracted to your husband? Or, let me correct that—ya see how you used to be attracted to him before you became the "frigid Bridget" you are today?

Well, that's how I am with my mate. Understand now? Probably not, but as my dad and your grandpa would say in Italian, "Tu no biaggia mei, ma ou solda fatta bonno, eh?" Which translated means, "You may not like me, but my money is good, huh?" And stop the bullshit about not wanting my money.

Hey, maybe I'll leave her a case of vanilla extract in my will or better yet, just one little bottle. How can you say you love me when you don't like anything that I am, don't like the adult business I own, don't accept gay marriage, and don't understand gay sexuality or bisexuality at all?

But people who "love" me don't think gay marriage is right, so I will spend the rest of my life alone and heartbroken just to satisfy their desires to keep marriage a sacred vow between a man and a woman. Adam and Eve, not Adam and Steve. Whaaa, whaaa, whaaa. Maybe that is why most gay relationships don't last.

Ya know what? Fuck you! And fuck your selfish beliefs. "Fuck fuck fuck!" as my Aunt Jenny, God love her, would say when she got mad. Now that was a real person. She never deserted my mother until her last breath, and I made sure I took good care of Aunt Jenny and her husband Uncle Frankie, even after Mom died.

Most of my family these days are so uneducated that they would pronounce diarrhea as diarear and point to their buttholes. So who in hell are they to judge me?

I expect people to be too smart and experienced; therefore, I am constantly disappointed in my fellow human beings. This has been true for all of my adult life, and I don't think I will ever be able to accept the truth of the matter.

Who are these people who claim to be my friends and love me and then pass judgment on me? I want the same life and joy that other people enjoy and take for granted. So put yourself in my shoes and ask yourself: if only gays could get married and they decided to outlaw all straight marriages, how would you feel?

The fact is that I want to be real and fair, and that is hard to do these days.

I wish people and the government would get out of our pants and bedrooms and give me the freedoms I fought for. I don't want middle-aged straight couples, most of whom have never fought for this country, to determine my future and life's path.

Hank, my ex, had a girlfriend who was born deformed (just as he liked it, because it made him look even more perfect than he already was). One day she called me a pedophile because Hank was only a month before his nineteenth birthday when we met. But she didn't mind all those dinners Hank paid for with my money where she ate up and pooped out my dinaro and ducats. Hank always picked the nasty, out-of-shape, ugly cabbage patch doll types so he would be the pretty one in the relationship and have more control over them.

I feel like the Jews did in the Nazi concentration camps who were viewed as subhuman and not of God. What ignorant little nasty bitches homophobic people are to think they're better than me because of one simple thing we do differently in bed. That's like saying, "Well, I eat chicken soup and you eat crème of mushroom, so I'm better than you."

After all the good things I've done in my life, the Christian and Jewish and animal rights charities I've given lots of money to, the poor people I've helped from all walks of life and of all colors, I'm then judged by Generation X and its nasty females who haven't done anything for anyone. It makes me wonder if there is any hope for diversity and individual rights in this world.

I feel there was more freedom back in the early '60s because nobody even knew me and therefore didn't judge me. I've even had old friends who found out recently about my sexuality and have proven to be prejudiced and intolerant about the important things in my life. These same people wouldn't dare object to equal rights of other so-called minorities, like women or blacks or the disabled.

Don't get me wrong—I know that I'm benefiting from new-age sexuality, but the family values that have been destroyed in the process doesn't make it worth it. Now you see how torn I am. A lot of people are doing everything with everybody, but they're so open, they don't really care about other people. They're spreading STDs like crazy. They're practicing unsafe sex and going home to their wives and girlfriends, and that's a violation of family values. I've benefited a lot from the greater openness around sex today. I'm not a leper anymore. Young men come on to me. But there has also been a price to pay.

I've given up on gay rights in my lifetime. Between the authorities not caring enough and gays going about it all the wrong way, I can't see mainstream America accepting us. The right way to achieve acceptance and equal rights is for gay people, especially gay men, to stay together in caring relationships for a reasonable length of time, like straight couples and many lesbian couples. Gays get bored too quickly—a bigger dick, a younger face, a fatter wallet, and they're down the road. They're like weather vanes. The slightest wind sends their attention in a new direction. I've had clubs where you couldn't get in the place, they were so jammed, and a year later you were lucky if you got a handful of people. My club was "tired" and "old" and "so *last year*." Next!

If you had gay couples who were together for more than ten years, who adopted and raised a child, who worked hard and paid their bills, who served in the military and got an honorable discharge as I did, I believe we'd be more accepted. But unfortunately, too many gay men see that as conforming or selling out to the straight community. A loyal partnership isn't something that straights invented. It's something God invented. If you love someone, you're with that person through thick and thin instead of worrying about the latest cute young boy or hot married man.

And yet I know how that life can take you away, because it is exciting. It's fun, it's fresh, and it's new. But how much of that can you do? When does it end? How much is enough? You can OD on sex as on anything else. I always had a much better time, in and out of bed, when I was with someone who was dear to me in a committed relationship. It was far more gratifying than ten minutes of sex with some stranger.

It really pisses me off that some straight, middle-aged, born-again couple with a combined IQ less than mine has more rights than I will ever enjoy. The hubby probably never spent any time in the military, while I went to war and risked my life for this country and our Constitution. And yet my country gives me no rights. Know what? They can all go to hell as far as I care, because I don't give a damn what they think of me.

Chapter 28:
Politics the Hard Way

Being a child of the Newark riots, I was angry and disgusted with the local political figures. They were the people who hired Dick Spina, the police director who raided the Waldorf cafeteria on a regular basis. And since I am a decorated Vietnam War vet, I didn't like how Kennedy and Johnson dealt with the military. The Vietnamese army was better supplied than we were. Therefore, I became a Republican.

I always had parade and funeral detail in the navy. There was an enormous contrast between watching the poor, sad families of dead sailors when we gave them the gun salute and handed them the flag that draped their loved one's coffin and the screams of anti-war protestors as we marched down the streets of Manhattan (that made me wish our guns were loaded). One time we were marching down the streets of New York, keeping step to "Anchors Aweigh," with protestors on one side of the street and supporters of the war on the other. As we approached the reviewing stand packed with admirals and generals and politicians, the music turned to "Ruffles and Flourishes." We marched so hard I felt the ground shake as tears filled my eyes.

These days I look at the contrast between the brave young people in the military who suffered for this country and those who voted (for the first time in their lives) for Obama. Now we have to rely on this so-called commander-in-chief of the armed forces who never served a day in the military nor ran a snow cone stand, to quote Karl Rove, to hold back the storm of militant Islam. I hope the young people who voted for Obama choke on their morning coffee, along with the potheads who voted for him hoping this administration would legalize marijuana so they can smoke it everywhere 24-7-365.

My political involvement lasted from the time I was discharged from the navy until recently, when I moved out of the Essex County area and up to the mountains of Morris County, New Jersey. The many years of my life I devoted to local, state, and national politics gave me mixed feelings because I never got any real money or jobs for my efforts. But the education I received and the opportunity to use my talents were worth it all.

I was involved in many elections on both the winning and the losing side—too many to remember, but a few really stand out as classic and exciting.

Tony Imperiale's race for the New Jersey state assembly was a classic and my real first taste of state politics. This was the one where we used the "start at the bottom" slogan to make the best of our rotten ballot position. The campaign was run on dollar and dime contributions from our local supporters, who gave us what they could afford, and Tony was infamous for talking local printers out of free signs and bumper stickers.

We never had more than a handful of workers at our headquarters, but we did whatever it took to get our message out to the voters. That meant distributing flyers door to door while at the same time removing our competition's flyers and signs. The locals supported us with pride, because they knew we were the reason they could feel safe in their homes and neighborhoods.

The best part was election night at Thom's Sorrento, a one-block square brownstone catering hall built years earlier by some local Mafia boss. As I came in from the districts I was working, the place was jammed with people screaming, "We're number one! We're number one!" Tony not only won an assembly seat but also came in first among all the candidates running for the two open seats. Those of us who worked in the headquarters every day wondered where all these people were when we needed them, but I found out this was the norm in most campaigns. A few people did all the work, but there were many others who wanted us to succeed but didn't want to be involved. The day after the election was the best because unbelievable numbers of new bumper stickers and house signs began popping up.

For the next election, the state Democratic Party and their Republican friends decided to chop up the districts to force Tony out of his assembly seat, so he decided to run for state senator as an independent from the new legislative district. That was a fun campaign, because we had to run it in many new towns, not just in the north and east wards of Newark.

I was put in charge of the Hudson County part of the new district where Imperiale was running. The Democrats in Hudson County weren't ready for our style of politics. We had more dirty tricks and games than they ever dreamed of. And they had never had such fierce competition. Every year, their supposed Republican "opposition" would make a deal and lay down like a prizefighter who got paid to take a fall. That way, the "losers" would get their piece of the pie. I found out through the years that this is the norm all over America. The party in charge has it made, and the "loyal opposition" is nothing more than actors playing out their part to get some nice crumbs.

Because of the tales of bravery and insanity we were known for during and after the Newark elections, the local party regulars were shivering in their shoes and afraid to take us on. Most of the party boys stayed away from us, and the labor union ass kissers who usually hung the local party signs got a taste of our rough and tumble style when they decided to get in a fight with one of our sign crews. The union people ended up in the hospital with their own posters stapled to their foreheads. Delicious!

The legends of our crazy deeds and mob connections hit the streets of Kearny and Harrison Secaucus and the postage-stamp town of East Newark. It was almost comical, but we knew that as long as they feared us, they would leave our signs and workers alone. One poor soul decided to try us out for size and firebombed our local headquarters one night after we were closed, so somebody firebombed his house with him inside. He and his wife survived, but he moved out of town the next morning. When the other loyal sheep heard of it, they decided not to try their luck with us again.

You needed to be cunning and shrewd and never let anyone scare you away. Once, some gay clown who was a big-time Democrat and hated our views called our headquarters and left messages to try to intimidate me. I went and had a "talk" with his stupid ass. Although he denied making the calls, I never got them again.

I found that fear was stronger than love, and respect more powerful than any street money the local parties would pass out on election day to buy votes. Of course, all this is in the book *The Prince* by Nicolo Machiavelli, but we didn't know about him until a few years later. That's when we found that Steve Adubato, the north ward Newark Democratic Chair, was a student of Machiavelli and carried a copy of *The Prince* in his back pocket. This only fueled our ethnic pride because this man from hundreds of years ago in Italy was still the respected godfather of politics. To this day, politicians from every background and from all over the world are smart enough to read and follow his beliefs.

We won the state senate race, and Tony went on to do some real good for our district and the state. But nobody remembers him or our cause because the world has changed into something I don't even recognize.

It wasn't long before I became a candidate for state office on the Republican ticket, which was a tough road to hoe in my district because it was big-time Democrat controlled. The truth of the matter is that nobody else wanted the slot in that heavily Democratic district. I got to learn the ins and outs of politics in my area and eventually across the country, and it has been my experience that the politicians control voters with menial jobs and nickel and dime programs, which keep people down.

The local Democratic chairperson, Steve Adubato, whose brother I ran against, spoke to me recently about my political involvement in the Newark area. Steve said I was the only gay/bi person who was ever accepted by that tough Imperiale crew. He said he didn't know how I did it and gave me a lot of credit for pulling it off. Actually, most people back then thought I was just interested in screwing guys and women and that I wasn't really gay at all. I wonder if they've got it more right than I do.

There was one young man in the Imperiale group who was as handsome as anyone I ever saw on or off the big screen and was well equipped also. This guy had a bad habit of having me over to his house under the false pretense of discussing the political situation. When I got there, he and his wife were usually in bathrobes, and I would wind up sandwiching him with his wife. We all had a ball. His wife was very pretty, and I don't know to this day why she tolerated it. But I guess she really loved him and wanted to keep him. I always wanted to do her too, but he never went for that angle.

I got major flak from a few gays who knew both the gay and political side of me, because it was anathema to be Republican and gay. That attitude is our biggest problem. Like blacks, gays only deal with and vote for Democrats, so how do you get anything done when the Republicans win? The other problem is that the Democratic Party takes gay voters, like blacks, for granted.

I will never again see the likes of the local Newark political machine. Of course, my brother Paulie and his mother-in-law, Rose, were right there getting their precious crumbs. Paulie and his kin were born to be Democrats because they were ignorant and desperate enough to be used and bought and sold for the benefit of the local party.

At one point Paulie ran for local Democratic district leader, challenging a man who had been the local district leader for over thirty-five years. I had been involved in local and state politics for quite a while by then but had never been involved in a Democratic primary race. The challenge came from north ward councilman Anthony Carrino, who was a perfect Democrat and decided to run in opposition to the district leaders, who were controlled by the north ward chairman, Steve Adubato. Ahh, what a delightful duo these two were. Adubato controlled most of the county's political positions and jobs, and Carrino had about five different city, county, and state jobs that he got paid for. I could never figure where he found the time to perform the duties and day-to-day work hours for them all. Just tireless, I guess. The Democratic answer to Superman.

Carrino met his Waterloo when he sold his political headquarters of many years to a Hispanic realtor, who then used it to run against Carrino. Ah, delicious. I have to give the devil his due, though, because Tony Carrino did endorse me when I ran for assemblyman against boss Adubato's brother, as did Tony Imperiale and many other local politicos. I didn't win but got so close that Boss A developed a lifelong vendetta against me because I had the audacity to run against "Saint Michael," his brother. You've probably seen Steve's son, Steve Jr., acting fair and balanced on TV, but like Dad, he's a true left wing liberal and a giant phony.

So Paulie "Connoli" asked me if I could help him in the election against the current leader, Purcell. The whole north ward honored and respected Purcell, because he was a Democratic district leader who for thirty-five years herded the cattle and sheep to the polls every year, as all the local parties did through district leaders like him. *Baaaahhhh! Moooooo!* Ya see, the longer you last at the top of the herd, the more rice and corn they dump into your trough.

Paulie was the perfect candidate for Democratic district leader, being angry, poor, and ignorant (oh yes, and desperate too).

So I ran his campaign the only way I knew how, and that was on a large scale. Although it was only one north ward district, you'd have thought he was running for mayor of Newark. During the weeks of electioneering that followed, every two-dollar crony who lived in the district, and even some from the surrounding areas, confronted us. That's because Boss Adubato ran every district race as if it were going to unseat him, and he knew that the loss of this particular seat, which he had controlled for such a long time, would be a black mark on his heretofore perfect winning record.

As a result, the battles that went on in the weeks before election were both horrific and comical. Drunken local losers and city and county employees rang Paulie's doorbell, begging or threatening him not to run. Election day was the war to end all wars. Paulie's "beautiful wife," who got flowers the day after election, rolled out of bed at three in the afternoon as usual. By then I had already thrown her friend Madeline, who was one of our own challengers, out of the polling place for telling undecided voters not to vote for my brother or the machine would jam.

As Madeline screamed and ranted, I called the board of elections on her stupid ass. I even made a song up for Paulie to the tune of "Mammy," but his wife didn't find the humor in it and walked away as I sang it. As luck and timing would have it we won, unseating the thirty-five-year Democratic district leader. Of course, Paulie Connoli had to ignore my warnings and scream at the top of his lungs, "*I won! I won!*" This infuriated Purcell's family, leading to a riot in front of the district polling place (which was loads of fun). Try to argue with a herd of ignorant sheep who've just been told their rice and corn ration will be cut off, or at least reduced substantially.

Okay, just for fun now and to the tune of Al Jolson's "Mammy," here's the song I believe Paulie's defeated opponent Purcell sang in his sleep.

> *Paulie, why ya runnin'? Why ya runnin'? Come on now, Paulie*
> *I'd give the world to see . . . you drop out now and throw your votes to me*
> Because I need them, oh I need them, how I need them . . . I . . . need . . . them, Paulie

The folks downtown won't pay me no more
And then I'll have to even the score
Paulie, Paulie, why don't you go play with your ballie?
Russo, Russo, please throw your votes to me, oh
Paulie, why ya runnin'? Why ya runnin'? Come on
now, Paulie
You know I need your votes
I'll buy you cars, cake, and three nanny goats
Why doncha listen? Snakes a hissin', cats a pissin'
I'm angry, Paulie
My own wife says that you're gonna win
And that would be a serious sin
Paulie, Paulie, I'll buy you a big box of Connoli
Russo, Russo, please do this thing for me, oh
Paulie, where ya goin'? Where ya goin'? Get back
here, Paulie
I'm gonna do a slow count to five, and then you'll
wish you weren't alive

During the course of that campaign, I battled with so many political sheep that I can't believe it was all about one lousy district. At one point, when some fat drunk came to Paulie's house and Paulie's wife pronounced this guy a close friend of theirs, I had the pleasure of throwing the drunken asshole down my brother's side steps and into a clump of bushes. Oh man, what a pleasurable feeling that was.

Of course, by the time election day rolled around, Tony "The Phony" Carrino and Adubato had made their deal, which left my brother and the rest of those running on Carrino's line high and dry during and after the election. Paulie's wife and mother-in-law blamed me as usual, sending me angry looks as I sat at his kitchen table, so I told Paulie to go and see Boss Adubato and make his own deal.

Paulie took my advice and spoke to Adubato, but of course he did it in his usual crybaby way of prostrating in front of the prince of the sheep. Paulie agreed to never run again, thereby securing him and his wife jobs in the county courthouse. As usual, his wife, Joann, couldn't get up before the crack of noon to report to work and was terminated shortly thereafter, and Paulie decided he didn't want to work there either.

I guess the whole election was a waste of my time, but I did get to defeat the sheep at their own game. Plus Paulie Connoli became this big, all-knowing numbers man guru in the local Dems eyes as he mastered the jargon. He even bullshitted Boss Adubato into believing that he was this professor of political science and vote god of the North Ward and had all these followers bowing at his feet.

Carrino and his crew decided to name me the lowliest of political prostitutes in Newark for helping Paulie win. Fact was that Carrino was the biggest political whore of all time, while Adubato was in the ruling class of Democratic political whores, and still is as I write this book. But that's what you have to be to get anywhere in local politics in New Jersey, which is the snake pit of Democratic politics.

There are countless towns and cities controlled by Democrats throughout America, and an iron fist rules them that nobody sees, unless they're part of the organization's ruling class or are unfortunate enough to lock horns with them. As Tony the Phony said to me as I tried to spare my brother from the wrath of the Dems at a local meeting, "You shouldn't be here, Danny. This isn't a political prostitute's meeting."

"Then why are you here?" I asked him.

Of course, he acted like he didn't hear me and went on with his pantomime farce of a meeting as one guy cried and said he was dying of cancer and another blabbered about losing his home. *Whaaa!* Anna Louttade Syndrome at its best.

Chapter 29:
. . . And More Politics

Recently, the local Essex County Dems appointed their election commissioners. The law states that they must appoint one from each party, so what do you think they do? They simply appoint a Republican commissioner who's in their pocket and will go their way in any disputed election. It's disgusting to see how blatant they are. This guy they appointed lives in a filthy, roach-infested house his mother left him and never did an honest day's work in his life. He has also collected checks from multiple Democratic state legislators. Some Republican, huh?

I struggled for years to pay my mom's bills and my own and never got one krona or rupee from any of the local politicos, who viewed me as a political maverick.

My dear friend Joe Lonzello said it best: "Show me a toilet, and the Democrats control it." And although Republicans aren't much better these days, when a Democrat wins he gives his brother a job, but when a Republican wins his brother doesn't need a job.

My brother's mother-in-law managed to go up my ass for many years. You see, like most losers, Rose was a puppet of the Democratic Party, and since I was always locking horns with them, she was born to go up my ass. She found a way to harass me and my mother for many years with whiny complaints and problems that annoyed us and tied up our time, which we then couldn't use for attacking her precious "party of the people." She also had a habit of crashing any political event I was attending and causing me embarrassment, which Paulie thought was cool as hell. He protected her, saying she was only exercising her right as a voter and a citizen. Like so many others, Rose had her head stuck in the public trough and did harm to anyone who got in her way.

I would see them with their pointy "line all the way" hats on election day, working hard for their party. Meanwhile, they got the day off from their jobs, paid by the city or county.

In later years we would go around with video cameras terrorizing them. We'd laugh out loud as they ran like thieves caught robbing a fruit stand or a poor box in a church, or maybe like roaches when you turn on the lights. To them, I was that "fucking Danny Russo" who wouldn't go away and leave them alone to do their "jobs," as they called them. They really believed it was part of their job description to work for the Democrats on election day, while the Republicans were worthless because the Dems paid them off to not show up at the polls. As they say, politics as usual.

These "leaders" and elected officials would show up at every wake, wedding, party, and event, like the local Italian feasts for one saint or another. I saw Ralph D., the Essex County sheriff and one of the nastiest and phoniest Republic rats, put a dollar on Saint Bartholomew (or Benny the Blade as we called the saint, because he held sword stabbing Satan in the head). Then the sheriff snuck around to the back of the statue to retrieve his lousy dollar, like a Labrador retriever hunting a bone. Here's a guy who has had a big job with the Democrats, after being defeated by Democrat John Cryan, who himself was eventually indicted and had to step down for robbing money from county employees, and Ralphie still goes to the local market for the bent can sale.

Ralphie boy could have had another term as sheriff on the Republicrat line, but his ego got in the way and he wouldn't pay off the hungry beast. So he lost to Cryan, and one phony replaced another.

Whores and thieves, gypsies, tramps, and losers. Give me your scum, your fools, your huddled asses yearning to screw thee. I light my lamp upon the golden trough. Now all the yuppies are liberals because they believe it's best for this country and "oh my goodness, the whole world," but they aren't considering their children's future.

But politics has always been this way and always will be. I remember when Tony Imperiale was being paid by the local politicians, both Democratic and Republican, to have poll workers at every polling place in Newark's north ward, but Tony had other plans for the money. How do you make it look like you have ninety-six paid poll workers when in reality there are only a half dozen in all?

That was the easy part. We had a station wagon with different disguises in the back, and we had the list of where the political bastards would be going to check up on us, so we preceded them to every polling place and changed into our disguises. We went from sunglasses to moustaches to accents, to make up and beards and hats and coats, screaming "Caputo" and "D'ambola Caputo" and "D'ambola" (the names of the two joke candidates) in a Spanish accent, as if we were selling tacos from a corner stand. All the while we passed out the politicians' cards. They bought it and paid Tony and we got a big laugh. We were all running around shouting "Caputo" and "D'ambola" for months after that election.

In those days we used to call election day "all souls day," because there were the white candidates in our areas of Newark and the black ones in the other wards. We knew that dead people and no-show voters were voting for the black politicos. In order to compete, we needed to do the same, so we had this conga line in front of the voting table and a list of dead people and those who hadn't come out to vote. When there was a half hour left for voting, we went into the booths and voted for them.

This still goes on today in the inner cities, which are now all black and Hispanic. They bring in their districts at over 100 percent, which is supposed to be impossible, but those inner city Dems have this magic way of getting more than the total number of registered voters to vote.

Once a young policeman was in the polling place, and he had a look of fear on his face, so I tried to comfort him by saying it goes on during every election. But it didn't seem to help calm his nerves at all. I made a play for him, which made him even more nervous, and eventually I told him to go get coffee. He jumped at the chance, as if I had any authority to tell him to leave.

Many polling places throughout the city always had big turnouts, which of course was impossible. Every candidate had their people involved, and we voted both on the right and the left. But these days in local politics it's all on the left, except for the federal elections where you can count on the local Democrats in power to steal it for their congressional, senate, and presidential candidates. It amazes me that they have been doing it for so long and nobody does anything about it. It has changed elections, like Kennedy/Nixon, which everyone admits was stolen by the mob and Chicago Mayor Daley. The Democrats and the mob have had this unholy alliance since World War Two. Kennedy won nationwide by one tenth of one percent.

Speaking of liars and thieves, later on in life my brother Paulie took his jargon-meister style of liar's politics to Bloomfield, the next town over from north Newark, where all of us had moved. Paulie was lucky to be on the Republican line because he happened to be in the right place at the right time. Of course, he was still an ignoramus from north Newark, a persona always supported by his wife and children, and let's not forget his mother-in-law, fall-and-sue-you Rosie.

The campaign was a farce from start to finish. Paulie could have easily won in Bloomfield, a town that went Republican even during Nixon's problems with Watergate. But *nooooooo*, he had to get his Newark anger and ignorance up. He tried to terrorize everyone else on the ticket with threats of going to the press and stepping down off the ticket, saying the Republicans in Bloomfield were a bunch of thieves and liars. I tried to talk to him, but his wife wouldn't let him listen to me, so I let him go down the toilet on his own and get defeated by an old parrot of a Democrat named E. Henry Tourto.

After Paulie lost, I started calling councilman Tourto, saying in my broken Italian that "tourto tu fatta no peddida forta forto," which translated meant he made very strong or powerful farts. Ha! The poor man had no idea what I was talking about, but it was funny as hell to everyone at our local political headquarters who listened in when I called him.

Tourto once died on the operating table election night, but as they revived him and brought him back, he actually won that election, too. We were thinking of eventually running him posthumously for governor to see if his luck would hold out.

Even dead he would do a better job than most of the assholes in office today.

Chapter 30:
Where Did the Years Go?

Mother's Day just passed, and I visited my parents' graves. I find it funny that Mom, who outlived my dad by about thirty-five years and was there to help with her grandchildren, didn't get flowers from anyone but me. There was not a flower or a note or a candle or even a tear. I don't need those cheap plastic flowers, and neither do Mom and Dad.

Where did the years go? Where did all the real people go?

Young people have no love for their families and forget their parents as soon as they're buried (or even before). Oh Momma, how I dreaded that day all my life, and when it finally came and you died in my arms, as I promised you would, I tried and failed to find a place where you weren't dead.

On that December 16, 1997, I remember hugging her and pressing my face to hers, crying, "No, Mommy, no." And as she left this earth, I got a message in her voice: "It's all right." That helped me for a while. Mom had been sick for many months before her death, and I knew it was about to happen, but the loss was so great that I mourned her passing for over ten years. And then there were the people who disrespected her by not showing up at her wake.

It was nine days before Christmas, Mom's favorite holiday, when I picked out her coffin. I got a very expensive and beautiful rose-colored coffin, with tiny roses engraved in the corners, because Mom's name was Rosaria or Rose. Remember my dog Beno and how I can't let go?

I found her a wonderful dusty rose gown in an elegant store in Nutley with shoes to match. And I got beautiful white—and rose-colored poinsettias that I placed around the base of the coffin. It was very nice and the last thing I could do for Momma.

There is, however, one regret I do have, which I will mention time and again. If I could do it all over again, I would have gotten a formal education and found that nice lady my momma was always wanting me to find, gotten married like many closeted guys did, and had lots of children. I'm not saying I could take the magic straight pill, but I now realize that I could have lived yet one more secret life and done well at raising a good family.

If I had my way, I would change the way people think about gays and not clump them all together in the same gold lamé room. I have tried throughout my life to be a good person and a good American, as have the majority of gay and lesbian Americans, but it seems we cannot be accepted because for a few times a week we do something different in the bedroom than the rest of America.

I guess I'm just a bitter and cranky old man. It seems that everyone wants you to die so they can take your money or possessions or even your job. Nobody really cares about your well-being. But they have forgotten the Golden Rule—he who has the gold makes the rules. Older people for the most part have the gold and the knowledge and therefore the power, like it or not. Sometimes you can just walk up to people with your weathered face and gray hair, and they don't even dare to trick you into something you don't need or try to overcharge you for fear you might bite their heads off.

I was always amazed at how many young guys liked sex with older guys and women, although they usually kept it secret. I always used to joke that there was hope for us in the future, and now I'm glad for it. Some really nice young guys are sincerely interested in older men. Sooner or later I'm going to claim one for my own. Someday my prince will come, or maybe my princess.

I'm seeing a beautiful young lady these days who knows about my sordid past and doesn't mind, as long as I'm "a good boy" from now on. I hope she really doesn't expect that from me. But who knows? Maybe I'll have the family I always wanted now that I'm an old man.

By living as long as I have, I've gotten so much better at just about everything in the last few years, because I've experienced everything many times before and know the right row to hoe well in advance. This is true in my politics, religion, business, personal relationships, and just about everything else as well, including my cooking. Older people are time machines of information, if you will only listen. Please absorb what they have to say so you can someday use their wisdom. Knowledge is power.

My life has been one of conflicting and contradictory emotions and actions, but I wouldn't want to change that now because therein lies my spice, drive, and excitement.

People who used to respect me for my intelligence and business sense are now calling me, saying they need to protect me because I'm this "nice guy that everybody uses." Oh boy, you know where that is leading. They think I'm getting senile and that maybe they can extract money from me. Boy, I can't wait for that crap to start so I can slap them down and show them how wrong they are about me. One dude just called and said, "Oh Dan, are you in that big house all alone? Aren't you scared?"

I said, "No, I'm not really alone. I have my fences and gates and dogs and alarms, and oh yes, I almost forgot, my legal guns that I keep loaded all around the house."

And I wasn't exaggerating. What a world to have to live like this today.

But whenever I get depressed, I can splash on certain colognes and feel better, almost like being back in Broadway Barbers with Vic and my shoeshine stand. It really lifts my spirits and makes me remember only happy and good times.

My advice is that if you're a man, be a real man and a total man. And if you're a woman, be a real woman and a total woman, no matter what your choices are in life, sexual or otherwise. Don't be an actor or an actress. Don't do what society expects of you. Don't be overly masculine or overly feminine. Don't be overly anything. Be yourself, whatever that might be. I see so many guys out there who could be normal people, but they're walking around with a lisp and a limp wrist, and it's unnecessary. I don't know what drives them to do that.

Back at the Waldorf, people weren't conforming to a role. They were being who they were. In those days, people were people. Everyone was real—more real than they are today. Ironically, because being gay was taboo, people were more honest. They weren't conforming to popular notions of being gay because there weren't any. They were just being themselves. Whatever it was, it was a lot better than what we have now.

And it was my love for that world that takes me back to downtown. It's 1963, and I'm in the Waldorf with Eleanor Roosevelt, Transistor Sister, Mad Alice, and the rest of my friends. We're sitting around drinking coffee, laughing together, and sharing the latest stories. We're all young, and the night has only begun.

The End

www.ingramcontent.com/pod-product-compliance
Lightning Source LLC
Chambersburg PA
CBHW020911290526

45784CB00002BA/501